The Historical Value of Myths

This book explores the connection between history and mythology by engaging with myths not as allegories or falsehoods, but as representations of historical experience. Historical approaches to myth are often absent from discussions of mythology, which favour symbolic and psychological interpretations. This analysis traces certain episodes of myths' complex ancestries, from when their relationship with history could not so easily be severed, to subsequent attempts, which misunderstood myths as confused, undeveloped lenses for humanity to view the world. Drawing on the works of English philosopher R.G. Collingwood and the Romanticism movement, the book argues for the expansion of methodological approaches to myths. It explores the ways in which myths have served as clues for the history of civilization and humanity's ever-changing complexities.

The Historical Value of Myths is an illuminating read for advanced undergraduates, postgraduates, and researchers in the fields of mythology, the philosophy of history, and anthropology.

John Karabelas is an independent researcher with interests in the philosophy of history and European cultural and intellectual history. He has published articles on R.G. Collingwood's philosophy ("Fairy Tales and Totemism," 2011; "Rationalism and the Law," 2015), and the philosophy of history of the British idealists (2018).

The Historical Value of Myths

John Karabelas

Routledge
Taylor & Francis Group

LONDON AND NEW YORK

First published 2023
by Routledge
4 Park Square, Milton Park, Abingdon, Oxon OX14 4RN

and by Routledge
605 Third Avenue, New York, NY 10158

*Routledge is an imprint of the Taylor & Francis Group, an informa
business*

© 2023 John Karabelas

British Library Cataloguing-in-Publication Data
A catalogue record for this book is available from the British Library

Library of Congress Cataloging-in-Publication Data
Names: Karabelas, John, author.
Title: The historical value of myths / John Karabelas.
Description: New York : Routledge, 2023. | Includes bibliographical
references and index.
Identifiers: LCCN 2022043843 (print) | LCCN 2022043844 (ebook) |
ISBN 9781138229891 (hardback) | ISBN 9781032440712
(paperback) | ISBN 9781315387703 (ebook)
Subjects: LCSH: Mythology--Historiography. |
Historiography--Philosophy. | History--Philosophy. |
Mythology--Philosophy.
Classification: LCC D16.9 .K3564 2023 (print) | LCC D16.9 (ebook)
| DDC 907.2--dc23/eng/20221018
LC record available at https://lccn.loc.gov/2022043843
LC ebook record available at https://lccn.loc.gov/2022043844

ISBN: 978-1-138-22989-1 (hbk)
ISBN: 978-1-032-44071-2 (pbk)
ISBN: 978-1-315-38770-3 (ebk)

DOI: 10.4324/9781315387703

Typeset in Times New Roman
by MPS Limited, Dehradun

To the memory of my mother
To my father
To Mafalda and Olimpia

Contents

Preface   ix

PART I   1

1   The enigma of myth as history: the view from antiquity   3
    Content, structure, and the import of myths 6
    Aristotle on the relation between poetry and history 10
    Final remarks and summary 11

2   The decadence of myth: "priestly lies", exaggerated
    histories, and allegories   17

3   The significance of method: R.G. Collingwood and
    fairy tales as myths   26
    The historical character of fairy tales 27
    The value of method 32

PART II   43

4   Romantic historiography and myths   45
    The meanings of Romanticism 47
    The historical mindedness of Romanticism 51
    Historical change 59
    Historical cosmopolitanism 64

viii   *Contents*

Unity of the mind and freedom 68
The emergence of Romanticism: the relationship between
  history and political philosophy 71

5   **Edmund Burke: the forgotten historian**   77

The historicity of myths: some thoughts on
history and myth   85

Index   98

Preface

This book is a study on some aspects of the historical value of myths. This aspect of myth is less understood than commonly believed and the historical approach is curiously absent even from general books that trace the history of mythology as a discipline and its various interpretations.[1] The situation is somehow better when it comes to books which cover the history of historical thought. There, usually through a more general presentation of culture, the connection between history and myth is examined but the treatment is unavoidably sporadic, limited, and fragmented. Perhaps next to the more well-known theories and interpretations of myths –allegorical, symbolic, anthropological, structuralist, psychological, and so forth– the historical approach may seem too pedestrian. Myths have a cryptic and elliptical quality, and this perhaps has favoured more fanciful and often outlandish explanations. Occasionally these approaches may have produced some serviceable suggestions and may have initiated useful discussions. But on the whole they have seriously misunderstood myths by either seeing them as something they are not or by refusing to engage candidly with them. To the extent that these interpretations have often been derogatory and sometimes "nothing less than chthonic,"[2] they have obscured any positive understanding of myth. The assumption in this book is the opposite: myths were not fanciful lies, symbols, or allegories but there was a sense of historical experience in them; in many respects they are the conceptual progenitors of history.

The difference between seeing myths as symbols, allegories, to stand "for" something and so forth, and seeing them as having a historical dimension, is substantial and methodologically intriguing. The emphasis on the concealed, the symbolic, the allegorical, and the covert supports an endlessly interpretative manner of enquiry that revolves around a-historical concepts. These attempts have had a long and varied existence throughout history, under various guises and postulated entities (stages of development, instincts, inner impulses, various unsubstantiated categories, etc.) which purport to capture the essence of reality and of human condition. They advance a view of reality replete with hidden structures and meanings, where forces operate beyond ordinary human discernment. It is a reality that can be decoded, unlocked to reveal the secrets of existence. Such interpretations are not endemic in the treatment of myths only but they extend to a wider area of cultural manifestations. They produce errors as they attempt to interpret culture and man by using non cultural coordinates and wrong categories of reference. These interpretations become obsolete and then return afresh, perpetuating thus a "history versus 'hermetic' traditions" game.

The historical answer to these interpretations is very different although not always clear, as history itself has been used as a vehicle to propagate such interpretations. When, that is, a historical enquiry is conducted under certain psychological, economic, political, sociological, etc. notions and categories. These categories are abstractions, at best they represent only one aspect of reality, but they attempt to interpret the whole reality under those terms. They have become interpretative micro-movements within history itself, but their relation with history is tenuous. This is an old and complicated problem and deep down a problem of method and general disposition. I have tried to discuss some of its features in the sections devoted to R.G. Collingwood and the historiography of Romanticism. With regard to the interpretation of myths the latter can be seen as a missed opportunity to advance a clearer understanding of their historical value, as it was predominantly the poetic and the philosophical dimensions of Romanticism which dealt with myth, not the historiographical. On the other hand Collingwood did not exhibit any hesitation dealing with this difficult material as historical evidence. His approach was bold and imaginative but also suggestive and credible. His work on the subjects of fairy tales and myth is very little known but it is still relevant and merits further attention.

The historical value of myths even inadvertently involves the relationship between myth and history. Because the question of the historical value of myths is not only if they could be used as artefacts to say something about the past and the societies which produced them. Usually there has been another sense attached to this mythical historicity, one that had followed myth from its early existence: could we stretch our evidential request to see those narratives as being, in some broad sense and special way, historically informative themselves and able to impart factual details about past events and persons? The first section of the book will try to understand why this question even became possible in the first place. It will examine some of the reasons for the relative predominance of the mythological perspective and also for the gradual loss of myth's ability to furnish a historically convincing explanatory vision.

The desire might exist to see the above decline through the myth to reason (from *Mythos to Logos*) trajectory, which has often been used to explain the European civilisation's *forward* movement. This usually implied a relatively steady, if not entirely unhindered, course away from superstitions, old beliefs and unsatisfactory tales, towards explanations that possess a markedly different way to account for reasons, motives, causes, and the like. Anything that did not quite support this course could be jettisoned, an inconvenient and embarrassing remnant of human folly and of our disposition towards bouts of irrationality. Nuanced and qualified versions of this view do exist[3] to remind us of Herbert Butterfield's warning against interpretations of human history where a linear cultural development usually involves following the upward adventures of an idea until it reaches a discernible maturity and final triumph. That things are infinitely more complicated is now a commonplace, albeit occasionally forgotten. Historical periods and events are not judged according to how well or ill could anticipate things to come. And the relationship between the old beliefs and the new beliefs is not one of necessary tension and ultimate substitution but of intricate interaction and overlapping identities.

In the aforementioned respect, myth's is not a straightforward story of dominance, decline, and resurrection, and its fate has been singularly turbulent. It is even doubtful whether myth ever recovered its initial position, which was certainly never quite one of unreserved acceptance. But at some point it did seem possible to purge myth from many of the negative layers it had accumulated. It was when some people began to talk more about historical method and understand the special character of history. These advances of history enabled a more receptive study of mythology, as they made clear that other elements of human experience may also become part of a proper historical enquiry. It was Vico and various aspects of Romanticism that shaped this new historical outlook. Romanticism placed emphasis on a genuine appreciation of past cultures and societies; it saw history as an autonomous, self-sufficient enquiry not a handmaid of the present; and by suspecting generalisations and extreme rationalism, it found something substantial and considered in individuality and in the particularity of judgement. It is not, therefore, surprising that in Romanticism we find the primary lines of the historicity of myths revived and redrawn. Vico, chronologically closer to the Enlightenment, had very little in common with the basic presuppositions of that movement and the mode of thinking of many of its exponents. He was in many respects a

Romantic thinker before Romanticism. It is not altogether obvious to what extent that new clarity made itself understood, as different forces were active while Vico and several Romantics were trying to make inroads into the historical thinking. The overriding concern of the pre Romantic period, from the Renaissance onwards, had been the advancement of a scientific spirit, often at the expense of the idiosyncrasies of the activities in the human sphere. In such intellectual surroundings a serious study of culture and myths could not progress far. Myths, in particular, were at variance with the prevailing spirit, they were oddities, vestiges of irrationality, a curious product of an unscientific, superstitious and credulous mind to warrant serious attention.

The relationship between history and myth has sometimes taken the form of an enquiry which has become known by the name of mythistory. What this name indicates is not always perfectly clear.[4] Often the conflation of the two terms might imply that a hybrid form exists which is not quite myth, not quite history. Assuming, that history is an enquiry closer to truth and myth the opposite of truth, the result is that this hybrid has commandeered history's repute in order to deceive us into accepting a semblance of truth, or perhaps quite simply to convince us that history is indeed myth, open to interpretations and counter interpretations that always lead to falsehood. To insist that the belief that truth is somewhere to be found is nothing more than an illusion. Here we enter the paradoxical and confusing domain of allegedly constructing, inventing, fabricating histories for all sorts of reasons: nationalistic aspirations, defining identities, glorifying the past, shaping various claims, and so forth. Although it is true that certain narratives may indeed create all these things, it is not clear why we would insist, by elaborately constructed explanations, on calling them history. In the end, the tendency of this approach is to see the entire life, reality, and the past as nothing but a spectacle or a series of misdirected actions. This tendency paints a consistently negative picture of strife, struggle, and conflict, while omitting or even ridiculing the positive aspects of life as something that denigrates or disguises the various infirmities. A different, more positive, meaning of mythistory may also be possible. This is the case, for instance, with McNeill, Kelley, and Mali.[5] Suggestive as their interpretations may be, the present study does not, most likely, contain enough to claim any similarity or identity of purpose with them.

Myth's relationship with history gives us some clues as to the nature of our civilisation, some of its features and transformations. And certainly some of its complexities. Myth is important as much for its complexity as for its revered position as humanity's first real voice. Its relation to history has been very strong and in some sense myth has helped history's intellectual development and self-realisation. In a way myth came first and paved the way for a clearer understanding of subsequent historical assumptions. In what follows the shifting and difficult landscape of the interpretation of myths is also used to give us an idea as to how far the boundaries of history can be stretched without becoming entirely distorted. If myths are arduous, inscrutable, and mysterious what is history to make of them? Can it cope with their explanatory demands or make any sense of their – assuming there is one – ultimate meaning? Myths challenge or even dilute (even more so than usual) history's ability to comprehend and explain, but as long as they constitute a genuine and communicable aspect of human experience, there is no reason why history will not be able to take on this challenge.

Notes

1 See for instance: Segal, *Myth: A Very Short Introduction*; Segal, *Theorizing about myth*: Csapo, *Theories of Mythology*; Thury and Devinney, *Introduction to Mythology: Contemporary Approaches to Classical and World Myths*. These are introductions to the study of myths and none of them makes any reference to a historical approach, and some of them have omitted any reference even to people like Vico. In Rose, *A Handbook of Greek Mythology*, various interpretative schools are discussed but the only one that may seem close to history is Euhemerism. In another relatively recent book, Witzel, *The Origins of the World's Mythologies*, Vico is briefly discussed but in the context of allegorical or Euhemeristic interpretations (Witzel, *World Mythologies*, 8, 21). Such treatment of the historical approach is not an aberration found only in these specific works but a common way to perceive the study of mythology, Even the recognition of a distinct historical approach seems frequently to be lacking.
2 Feldman and Richardson, *Rise of Modern Mythology*, xxiv.
3 See for instance Most, "From Logos to Mythos," 25–47.
4 In this respect, Mali has an informative chapter "Where Terms Begin: Myth, History and Mythistory" (Mali, *Mythistory*, 1–35).
5 Kelley uses the term "mythistory" in connection with the so-called Romantic historicism (Kelley, *Mythistory*, 3–20). There the element of construction through the use of language and symbol seems to be the main driving force. Also McNeill, *Mythistory*, 3–22; Mali, *Mythistory*, 1–35.5.

References

Csapo, Eric. *Theories of Mythology*. Oxford: Blackwell Publishing, 2005.
Feldman, Burton, and Richardson, Robert D. *The Rise of Modern Mythology, 1680–1860*. Bloomington: Indiana University Press, 1972.
Kelley, Donald R. "Mythistory in the Age of Ranke." In *Leopold von Ranke and the Shaping of the Historical Discipline*, edited by Georg G. Iggers and James M. Powell, 3–20. Syracuse: Syracuse University Press, 1990.

Mali, Joseph. *Mythistory. The Making of Modern Historiography.* Chicago: The University of Chicago Press, 2003.

McNeill, William Hardy. *Mythistory and Other Essays.* Chicago: The University of Chicago Press, 1986.

Most, Glenn W. "From Logos to Mythos." In *From Myth to Reason? Studies in the Development of Greek Thought,* edited by Richard Buxton, 25–47. Oxford: Oxford University Press, 1999.

Rose, Herbert Jennings. *A Handbook of Greek Mythology. Including its extension to Rome.* 3rd edition revised. London: Methuen & Co Ltd, 1945.

Segal, Robert A. *Theorizing about Myth.* Amherst: University of Massachusetts Press, 1999.

Segal, Robert A. *Myth: A Very Short Introduction.* Oxford: Oxford University Press, 2004.

Thury, Eva M., and Devinney, Margaret Klopfle. *Introduction to Mythology: Contemporary Approaches to Classical and World Myths.* Oxford: Oxford University Press, 2016.

Witzel, E. J. Michael. *The Origins of the World's Mythologies.* Oxford: Oxford University Press, 2012.

Part I

1   The enigma of myth as history: the view from antiquity

The birth of historical consciousness in ancient Greece, and to a large extent in Europe too, is a story of frequent amalgamation with myth, and gradual, but perhaps never total, release from its tutelage. History as a distinct activity grew, like many other fields of activity in ancient Greece, in an atmosphere imbued with myth, a vital ingredient without which, it has been argued, the Fathers of History "could never have begun their work."[1] In a sense it would have been close to impossible to distinguish those events and persons that belonged to history proper from those that belonged to myth proper. Even what was history proper and what myth proper would have been hard to define in mutually exclusive terms. From our point of view (when myth was already a strange and remote spectacle and not a quotidian reality any longer) the proximity between history and myth would seem to suggest a great opportunity for ancient historians to sharpen their methodological acuity. To do so would depend not so much on their willingness to separate the two but on their ability to do quite the opposite: to consider what it means when one distinct activity is so intricately linked to another. That this must have been the case, in an embryonic stage perhaps, is rather evident if we think that the tension between the two activities was never truly resolved by the Greeks. What we usually find is either a covert acceptance of myth as historically useful, or a hesitant dismissal of its historical value, sometimes these two attitudes would coexist within the same author. Carefully distancing themselves from an unequivocal and steadfast judgement on the relation between the two activities, those historians left a convoluted and interesting legacy. Whether as a problem of unresolved tension about boundaries or, more interestingly, as a question of meaning and function of history and myth, this legacy, often unwittingly and under several guises, was behind some substantial advances in the historical conception

DOI: 10.4324/9781315387703-2

from the eighteenth century onwards. History was helped to life by myth and has remained somehow indebted to it ever since.

* * *

The knotty relationship between myth and history had real consequences for subsequent historians. Even when the discipline of history had in the nineteenth century achieved methodological vigour, the treatment of the early phases of Greek history, enveloped as they were in uncertain origins that only myth purported to explain, presented some serious challenges. In dealing with these issues the metaphor of the curtain or the veil became a common theme among several historians of that period. Jacob Burckhardt, for instance, asserted that heroic myth "separates this world of remote antiquity from that of history, sometimes only as a thin veil, sometimes as a solid dense curtain."[2] Despite this precarious situation between myth and history, Burckhardt was under no illusion that what lies beyond that curtain or that veil can not "penetrate to us as actual historical facts."[3] Still for the ancient Greeks the mythical element had "a bearing upon the remotest times" and authors of "every period ... saw everything in a mythical way", albeit this was a process understood and expressed in ways which encouraged interpretative liberties.[4]

George Grote, in defence of his decision to separate the early parts of Greek history (legendary Greece) from the later periods (historical Greece), explained, using the same imagery, that it is not possible to "undraw the curtain and disclose the picture [of the legendary times]" because the "curtain *is* the picture ... the curtain conceals nothing behind, and cannot, by any ingenuity, be withdrawn."[5] Although Grote's determination to divide Greek history into those two compartments may have been a revolutionary conclusion for its time,[6] it was still not based on regarding the mythical parts as entirely devoid of historical sense or historical value. Grote simply admitted that the task of finding a satisfactory way to separate history from myth was not something that he was able (or even willing) to undertake on the basis of the available evidence.[7] Thus he described the early, legendary parts of Greek history without any presumption of "how much or how little of historical matter these legends may contain"[8] but also without ever denying that those early Greek legends may indeed "contain a good deal of history."[9] No doubt separating the past in such a way could not have been a very neat affair. More like a convenient method to get out of the way any spurious assertions, that may have appeared so to Grote, and pay fuller attention to what could be more safely regarded as history proper. Grote must have been aware that by merely describing the legendary past, instead of historically dissecting it, significant historical information could be lost. But this sacrifice was thought to be a reasonable enough methodological call.

Barthold Georg Niebuhr, discussing the early part of the history of Rome, also spoke of the 'many-coloured veil' which poetry had "flung ... over historical truth."[10] Examining the sources of ancient Greek history he was sceptical about "dragging into history" mythological elements and about trying to draw historical inferences from those elements.[11] He thought that for the historian the "whole region of mythology is extremely dangerous" and he argued against any belief that mythology may lead to "historical truth and certainty."[12] At the same time he was reluctant to exclude too many things, referring mainly to mythological things, from ancient history, also knowing that these were exactly the sort of things that will "always remain very obscure."[13] Despite his ambivalence Niebuhr's contribution to the "historical study of myth, barbarism, and oral culture ... has been a permanent feature of the study of history."[14]

From the aforementioned historians we get a sense of a more general difficulty which would frustrate everyone attempting to draw an elegant line separating neatly and unambiguously history from myth. Scepticism towards myths could exclude potentially valid historical information. Leniency towards them could produce a historical picture hopelessly unverifiable. It seemed that myths do not themselves (always) represent unquestionable and authentic historical events, but there was something more to them, they can not be dismissed altogether. They may be used as historical evidence only if we knew how to extract what is useful in them and jettison what is not. Any reasonably competent historian could be able to detect mythical elements that were absurd, outlandish, something that can not be history. But there could equally be other mythical episodes where such confidence would seem misplaced. It was the basic structure of epic poetry and myth that would make the historical boundaries too elastic. Within a mythical framework where some stories clearly could not possibly have been describing historical events, some had a convincing historical basis, and some were evasive and ambiguous, we would need to account for such fluctuations of function and meaning. A very strict and rigid juxtaposition between history and myth, the former being pretty much a truthful narrative, the latter pretty much a fantastical story, leaves many things hanging, unanswered. As it has been pointed out the entire affair often came down to what can be seen as a form of contest where "one kind of retelling of the past was being measured against another."[15] Those competing interpretations were not, however, necessarily hostile to each other (although occasional conflicts did arise) and they retained their individual validity as they coexisted side by side during the course of antiquity. This is another indication of the "artificiality of the sharp break" which is sometimes assumed between mythical and other forms of thought (historical, philosophical etc.)[16] The convenient evolutionary view from *mythos* to *logos* has still various anomalies to overcome. It is also important to remember that conceiving myth, especially heroic myth, as history was not something that occurred at a later point in Greek history but was prevalent throughout antiquity.[17] Most Greeks thought it quite apparent that heroic mythical stories referred to a past historical reality which could be discovered in those stories or "reconstructed from them."[18] The historical reality of the mythical past was not only a common conception among the Greeks but often the starting point of many ancient historical works.[19] In effect ancient historians thought of myth and history not in strict opposition but as "belonging to a single continuum."[20] Even the soberly rational Thucydides, although exercising caution and casting doubts on certain of the details, he nonetheless accepted myth as history and on the whole he was much more reliable than Herodotus about the historicity of myths.[21] To regard myth as history did not mean that myth had been absorbed by history. If anything, it would be more challenging to understand how history had actually managed to affirm itself against such a popular and ancient competitor.

Content, structure, and the import of myths

The Greek myths exhibit certain structural and content related peculiarities which make them convincing and believable as truthful narratives of historical events. When contrasted with other mythical traditions, for instance, the majority of Greek myths were unusual in dealing with heroes and heroines who occupied a specific time in the past. Although those characters had, alongside their virtues and vices, unusual powers they were not gods but humans and so were their actions.[22] These heroic figures, mythical as they were, in a way were also historical since "they show us the changing phases of the inner life of the Greeks, of which we would otherwise know nothing."[23] Also, as a rule, the Greek mythical events were not prone to the eccentric and the fantastical found in other traditions, but depicted exaggerated versions of life as we actually know it. The realistic and anthropomorphic character of myth has, to a certain extent, to do with the fact that "in the archaic period, heroic myth took the fixed form of epic poetry" which constructed a mythical realm closer to historical and quasi historical categories.[24] This aspiring realism, "a distinctive feature of Greek mythical narration in general"[25] and the anthropomorphic world, where monsters are rare and the fantastical elements subdued, attach a recognisable human and humane dimension to Greek myth and may explain its enduring attractiveness and its "immense impact ... from antiquity to the present day."[26]

These very characteristics (realism and anthropomorphism) have also been seen as a puzzling fact, a "considerable stumbling-block to modern general theories of mythology."[27] For it may be argued that any theory which attempts to interpret myths as bizarre stories that transcend known norms and reality, will have to use certain categories to support allegorical interpretations and explain those bizarre elements. But such categories will not be applicable if the mythical characters and the mythical events are closer to life and thus, in a sense, closer to history too. Where the element of realism is present and the fantastical elements recede, allegorical explanations become weaker, although by no means altogether implausible. Moreover, if anthropomorphism and realism are the norm, and the deviation from ordinary life's routines and conventions is slight, this deviation could very well be a matter of degrees: not so easily attributable to excesses of reason and the like, but to an exaggerated or caricatured version of some past events, or to a misremembered piece of history and so forth. In short incidents that may leak across the borders of history proper. This proximity of myth to history is a vital element as it defies easy and categorical explanations with regard to the function or functions of the mythical narrative. A-historical theories of myths, therefore, may always find it difficult to define boundaries between realistic and truthful narratives and more fictional ones, or almost impossible to deny a closer connection between history and myth, however complicated this connection may have been.

Not only were those mythical stories realistic and about human deeds, but they also did so within a framework of time which could be quite specific. The mythical period had a structure lending itself to the creation of a past that "could be dated and fitted in with history",[28] it was a universe arranged "in accordance with chronological – "historical" – criteria."[29] The chronological order was genealogical in structure and was achieved by synchronising genealogical information and thus interlinking the mythical stories. Alongside the mythical genealogies of the heroic period, the incorporation of historically real ones in the mythical narration helped to bridge the gap between the end of the mythical period and the beginning of history known through documents and memory.[30] The past became less vague and indistinct, something much more than just a non present. It could place its stories within establish-able time boundaries, as specific as the various genealogies permitted, and would enable a mythical narrative to resemble, or be transformed into, a historical one. What is also of interest is that the chronological development was the work not only of the early Greek historians but also of epic bards whose systematisation of the mythical episodes contributed "to the rationality of mythical narration in epic poetry."[31] It seems, therefore, that it was within myth itself that categories and components had already been ushered in which were to be, later on, associated almost exclusively with history. Historical categories such as realism and time specific chronology had been established and used by a historical turn of mind which was not history proper yet. History may have found those categories ready to use from myths. In matters of structure chronology was, perhaps, a far more important conceptual achievement than realism. Time is a necessary and essential characteristic of any historical narrative, and although time alone can not change an ordinary narrative into a historical one, a mythical narrative which operates within conditions of time becomes very convincing. Having realised the importance of time and specific chronology, myth was stretching and blurring the legitimate bounds of the past. The fact is that if myths were only fanciful and imaginative stories, they had gone to great lengths and it took a lot of effort just to imitate something they were not by assuming the cloak of a truthful narrative. If they only aspired to telling a good story, realism, anthropomorphism and chronology would have seemed superfluous ornaments. But with myths, especially Greek myths, there is always a lingering feeling that they were trying to do something more than simply offering a good story.

Besides any structural and contextual similarities with history, the peculiar value of Greek myths is clear from their importance and presence in almost every aspect of Greek life. From poetry, history and philosophy to visual arts and beyond, myths persisted for very long in a society which by all accounts had been quite advanced.[32] Ancient Greek society achieved a high level of sophistication and complexity and still believed in myths. Even if myths had their origins in an era of inventive poetical reflection when imagination and vivid pictures dominated expression, their subsequent persistence (somehow modified but always retaining aspects of their authority), after other forms (for instance philosophy and history) of making the past and the reality intelligible had assumed maturity, testifies to a phenomenon that acted almost as a building block in ancient Greek mentality. In the case of Greece, the not uncommon assumption that myths belong to a relatively crude stage of societal development and are supported by a naïve, gullible, primitive, and unsophisticated mind, is substantially weakened.

The mythological origins and the mythical traditions could still in historic times burden individuals and entire families, to the extent that they were prepared to avenge "wrongs suffered in prehistoric times" and to accept responsibilities for curses or ill-fate which could allegedly be traced back to their mythical ancestors.[33] What made people willing to encumber themselves in such a way and take seriously commitments in obedience to imprecise and nebulous commands of the past, can not easily be attributed to irrational modes of thinking or even to mere adherence to tradition. Those people believed their duties to be real because certain beliefs and forms of life exercised a powerful and credible influence on them. Myths must have meant more to those people than a fanciful story. It may be, of course, debatable whether the past had indeed left such obligations or whether a clear line of some grievance could be traced back to an original source, but for the Greeks the "mythological or sacred origin of many outer forms of life ... was felt to be very near."[34]

Where the closeness between myth and history assumes rather unequivocal dimensions is before the fact that at least some myths did contain useful historical information. They depicted or recorded actual historical people, places and events, corroborated by subsequent archaeological or more advanced historical research. Sometimes this information is available in a transformed and distorted way or discernible as survivals in myths of archaic customs and traditions. An interesting example of a possible survival of an ancient custom in myths is the story of the famous contest between Athena and Poseidon over the guardianship of Athens. Athena won because of the votes of the women that outnumbered those of men, and as such this episode may be taken as suggestive of a period when perhaps women may have had full citizenship and could vote.[35] It is often far from easy to tell with certainty how close to historical facts this and similar stories may have been. But myths offer tantalising glimpses into potential earlier stages of social organisation whose actuality is rendered quite convincing by the mythical narrative itself.

Challenging as it were to corroborate the historical evidence contained in myths or readily accept myth as history, scepticism became widespread. Such scepticism towards the historicity of myths was already present in antiquity among historians. But as the attitude of the Greek historians towards myths was ambivalent, so their scepticism was relatively mild. Myths could be used as historical material but they could not be trusted entirely. That myths are used in a certain way presupposes a certain conception of history and their history was advanced enough to be able to say that myth is not history but also not altogether alien to it. Thus scepticism never became total rejection of the mythical past. Sometimes scepticism would take the form of trying to iron out some of the more fanciful details by offering rationalistic explanations and thus risking damaging the delicate balance and the fabric of the myth. Hecataeus of Miletus, one of the important early historians or logographers, who is regarded as "the first Greek who admitted that he found Greek mythology 'funny'"[36] did offer such rationalistic explanations. At the same time he also "recorded mythology with a confident purity of tone."[37] Myths created contradicting and confusing responses and while recognising the absurdity of some of the legends, historians would still try to offer explanations essentially rehabilitating myths as a historically trusted source. Moreover, the alignment of the mythical and the historical pasts through chronology was so believable that not only allowed myths to resemble history but also made the opposite possible: to have, that is, "historical events expressed in the form of mythical narratives."[38] In many cases logographers and historians saw myths as a problem to solve, a problem which presented them with difficulties perhaps as serious as those of any other material that may have used in their historical work.

Aristotle on the relation between poetry and history

One of the most characteristic and well known illustrations of the complex and long standing relationship between myth and history in antiquity, is to be found in Aristotle's famous comparison, in his *Poetics,* between poetry and history to the effect that the former is more philosophical than the latter. Why Aristotle thought it reasonable to compare the two had nothing to do with any desire to defend poetry against the famous Platonic criticism.[39] Poetry could not possibly assume a more dignified status by being compared with history. From a philosophical point of view, one shared by both Plato and Aristotle, history was not held in high regard in antiquity because it was the enquiry which concerned itself with the particular not the universal and the general. In fact poetry, because of its universal aim, was more philosophical than history, and thus in a sense superior. But this was a feeble victory. Poetry was more philosophical but still below philosophy in the hierarchy of the arts.

What Aristotle was doing in comparing the two fields was simply to acknowledge a social reality and trying to work out some of its consequences. The reality was that both history and almost all forms of poetry drew their material from a past where the mythical and the historical elements were not clearly distinguished. Mythological events, according to the conception of the ancient Greeks, belonged to the past too and were used indiscriminately as historical facts to inform the composition of poetic or historical works. An accomplished tragedian such as Aeschylus would move freely between mythical and historical figures, between, for instance, Achilles and Xerxes and Agamemnon, and this may only seem surprising to us if we "misunderstand the twin facts that the Greeks regarded myth as history and that Aeschylus treated history as myth."[40] Poets and historians alike did not really question whether any difference between mythical and historical events existed. It was thus not "surprising that history should have been discussed and judged in antiquity, should have been measured, against poetry. ... For there must be no misunderstanding about one thing: everyone accepted the epic tradition as grounded in hard fact."[41]

It is against this cultural background that Aristotle's comparison between poetry and history may be understood. He links them through the common material they use (the past with both its mythical and its historical elements) and also through how each would treat that material. Poets would interpret their material more freely in order to support and elaborate the more comprehensive concerns of their craft. They would emphasise the internal logic of the events as to add to them potentiality and necessity and thus universalise their narrative. History, on the other hand, would strive to unite specific past events and achieve understanding of those event only, with no aspirations to ultimate or teleological interpretations. The particularity of the historical function and the universality of the poetical would, for Aristotle, mean that poetry is closer to philosophy. However poetry's universality could be attained by delving into a body of material which was not entirely reputable, since it did include bizarre tales and legends, hardly a reliable foundation for certainty and truth. This was one of the reasons why poetry was thought to be inferior to philosophy and why Plato criticised it so severely. In effect neither poetry nor history could be trusted and could not be considered real forms of knowledge. Aristotle's comparison, however, is invaluable in dissecting the relationship of the two and demonstrating that a special sort of kinship between myth and history has indeed been a quite old practice.

Final remarks and summary

Myths, especially epic myths, operated within a reasonably lucid framework of time and chronology with synchronised genealogies that eventually bridged the gap between the mythical and the historical periods. This was a process which began even before history proper, by mythographers and genealogists who "turned epic material into prose and ... thus codified and rationalized the legendary history of Greece."[42] The mythical world was mostly realistic and anthropomorphic, an exaggerated version of life instead of an entirely fantastical universe. Logographers and historians would have had an ambiguous attitude towards the mythical stories. The work of Hecataeus was predominantly about the mythical past, while Herodotus and Thucydides did cover historical events that fell within living memory but also dealt with earlier periods where the use of myths was inevitable. Other historians, such as Ephorus and Theopompus, "two of the most influential historians of antiquity ... rejected the narrow 'Thucydidean' criteria for the selection of subject matter" and were adamant about their willingness to include myths in their narratives.[43] In general ancient historians did not really question the feasibility of establishing the truth of the remotest past times and thought that despite problems, challenges and limitations it was possible to also use myths to do so. Perhaps it was an understandable enough desire to have such stories revered and validated, as they can pierce the mundane everyday with heroic and marvellous deeds. Those myths and stories would also provide for the later Greeks the only glimpses to their early history, which would otherwise remain entirely inaccessible. Moreover myth was, up to a point, a product of tradition, a story which was handed down mainly by non written narrative forms and no one person could be identified as the creator of any of those stories. People, thus, become even less prepared to readily jettison their traditional stories as pure fabrications. Not only the passage of time had made those stories venerable; they would also embody the collective knowledge and reason of past generations, in many ways a more reassuring sign of trustworthiness and reliability than single authorship.

The topic of myths in Greek antiquity is a vast one and in this section only a few basic features were examined, always focusing on the complicated relation between history and myth. Myths sure enough have been seen in other ways too. Certain myths could, for instance, assume the familiar political function of legitimising a certain claim. It is not always clear why this should be considered a function of myth and not of covert propaganda or of an elaborately constructed rhetorical programme. Perhaps the residual assumption is that myth can fulfil this function because it has the ability to support any such claim *historically*. Such a myth is to be believed because it can be conceived as having the appearance of a truthful depiction of past events. And at the same time as pseudo-history or something less than history and thus to distort irrevocably the access we may have to the past. Even this uncharitable view of myths reveals how inescapable any discussion about their historicity really is.

But there is always a danger with a thing possessing several functions and identities. Its descriptive categories may come under strain and suspicion: has myth not become merely a term of convenience under which a great many phenomena are made to fit and thus explained away? If myth is not something more than such an expedient accumulation of curiosities, we may reasonably begin to wonder whether our understanding of myth is deficient. At the same time this may also be an indication of myth's comprehensiveness, an all-encompassing explanatory structure that went beyond simply bringing the past closer by providing a plausible account of peoples and societies. In fact it has been argued that one of myth's main functions has been "to make the past intelligible and meaningful by selection, by focusing on a few bits of the past which thereby acquired permanence, relevance, universal significance."[44]

The interpretative difficulties are quite evident by the large number of methods having being employed to explain myths and by the extremely diverse and often conflicting accounts that the same material has produced.[45] It would be fair to conclude that certain myths may be beyond our capacity to understand and that "to grasp for 'the' meaning may be as hopeless as to grasp the evanescent shadows of the dead."[46] That is not to say, however, that what is true for some myths is true for all. And it may be that what had been in many cases missing was a correct method. What is more, from the picture we have tried to build in this section it has become clear that myths are not the product of irrationality or of the inability to distinguish between historical and non-historical conceptions and thus hopelessly confusing the two. Why then so many interpretations and theoretical approaches have distorted the proper nature of myths by offering convoluted, allegorical explanations and often belittling myths as a creation of an immature historical development? And why have these approaches largely ignored the connection between myths and history? The following section will attempt to trace, in rather broad strokes, the fate of myths and to understand how they became for centuries entangled with disparaging interpretations and try to see why this happened. The partial restoration of myths later on as something more truthful and historically trustworthy, largely depends on understanding why their decline has occurred in the first place. Their revival is in a sense linked to a reaction against certain modes of thinking and some enduring and recurring methodological errors.

14   *Part I*

Notes

1 Finley, "Myth, Memory and History," 13.
2 Burckhardt, *Greeks and Greek Civilization*, 136.
3 Ibid.
4 Ibid., 15.
5 Grote, *A History of Greece,* vii-viii.
6 Momigliano, "George Grote and the Study of Greek History," 63.
7 Ibid.
8 Grote, vii.
9 Momigliano, "George Grote and the Study of Greek History," 63.
10 Niebuhr, *The History of Rome*, 1.
11 Niebuhr, *Lectures on Ancient History*, 195.
12 Ibid., 196.
13 Ibid.
14 Kelley, *Versions of History*, 499.
15 Finley, "Myth, Memory and History," 14.
16 Segal, "Archaic choral lyric," 179.
17 Graf, *Greek Mythology*, 140.
18 Ibid., 121.
19 Ibid.
20 Ibid., 123.
21 Ibid., 122. Also Finley, "Myth, Memory, History," 14 and 18.
22 Griffin, "Greek Myth and Hesiod," 83; Graf, *Greek Mythology*, 141.
23 Burckhardt, *Greeks and Greek Civilization*, 155.
24 Graf, *Greek Mythology*, 141.
25 Ibid.
26 Ibid.
27 Griffin, "Greek Myth and Hesiod," 84.
28 Ibid., 91.
29 Graf, *Greek Mythology*, 140.
30 Ibid., 125-30.
31 Ibid., 126.
32 Griffin, "Greek Myth and Hesiod," 84.
33 Burckhardt, *Greeks and Greek Civilization*, 25-26.
34 Ibid., 25.
35 Jones and Pennick, *History of Pagan Europe*, 10.
36 Dodds, *The Greeks and the Irrational*, 180.
37 Levi, *Greek Literature*, 112.
38 Graf, *Greek Mythology*, 135.
39 Sykoutris, "Introduction," 69.
40 Winnington-Ingram, "Aeschylus," 283.
41 Finley, "Myth, Memory, History," 14.
42 Immerwahr, "Herodotus," 430.
43 Connor, "Historical writing fourth century and Hellenistic period," 464.
44 Finley, "Myth, Memory and History," 13.
45 A good example of this attitude can be found in Griffin, "Greek Myth and Hesiod," 94-95, where two versions of the myth of Adonis are shown to support strikingly different interpretations.
46 Griffin, "Greek Myth and Hesiod," 96.

References

Burckhardt, Jacob. *The Greeks and Greek Civilization*, Edited by Oswyn Murray, translated by Sheila Stern. New York: St Martin's Press, 1998.

Connor, W. Robert. "Historical writing in the fourth century B.C. and in the Hellenistic period." In *The Cambridge History of Classical Literature, I: Greek Literature*, edited by Patricia Elizabeth Easterling and Bernard MacGregor Walker Knox, 458–471. Cambridge: Cambridge University Press, 1985.

Dodds, Eric Robertson. *The Greeks and the Irrational*. Berkeley, Los Angeles, London: University of California Press, 1951.

Finley, Moses Israel. "Myth, Memory and History." In *The Use and Abuse of History*, by Moses Israel Finley, 11–33. New York: The Viking Press, 1975.

Graf, Fritz. *Greek Mythology. An Introduction*, Translated by Thomas Marier. Baltimore and London: The John Hopkins University Press, 1993.

Griffin, Jasper. "Greek Myth and Hesiod." In *The Oxford History of Greece and the Hellenistic World*, edited by John Boardman, Jasper Griffin and Oswyn Murray. Oxford: Oxford University Press, 1991.

Grote, George. *A History of Greece. From the earliest period to the close of the generation contemporary with Alexander the Great*. Vol. I. New Edition. London: John Murray, 1888.

Immerwahr, Henry Rudolph. "Herodotus." In *The Cambridge History of Classical Literature, I: Greek Literature*, edited by Patricia Elizabeth Easterling and Bernard MacGregor Walker Knox, 426–441. Cambridge: Cambridge University Press, 1985.

Jones, Prudence, and Pennick, Nigel. *A History of Pagan Europe*. London: Routledge, 1995.

Kelley, Donald R. *Versions of History from Antiquity to the Enlightenment*. New Haven and London: Yale University Press, 1991.

Levi, Peter. *A History of Greek Literature*. Middlesex: Viking, 1985.

Momigliano. Arnaldo. "George Grote and the Study of Greek History." In *Studies in Historiography*, by Arnaldo Momigliano, 56–74. London: Weidenfeld and Nicolson, 1966.

Niebuhr, Barthold Georg. *The History of Rome*. Vol. I. 2nd edition. Translated by Julius Charles Hare and Connop Thrilwall. London: Taylor, Walton and Maberly, 1831.

Niebuhr, Barthold Georg. *Lectures on Ancient History, From the Earliest Times to the Taking of Alexandria by Octavianus*. Vol. I. Translated by Leonhard Schmitz. London: Taylor, Walton and Maberly, 1852.

Segal, Charles. "Archaic choral lyric." In *The Cambridge History of Classical Literature, I: Greek Literature*, edited by Patricia Elizabeth Easterling and Bernard MacGregor Walker Knox, 165–201. Cambridge: Cambridge University Press, 1985.

Sykoutris, Ioannis. "Introduction, text and interpretation." In *Aristotle's Poetics*, edited by Ioannis Sykoutris and translated by Simos Menardos. Athens: Academy of Athens, Greek Library, 1937.

Winnington-Ingram, Reginald Pepys. "Aeschylus." In *The Cambridge History of Classical Literature, I: Greek Literature*, edited by Patricia Elizabeth Easterling and Bernard MacGregor Walker Knox, 281–295. Cambridge: Cambridge University Press, 1985.

2 The decadence of myth: "priestly lies", exaggerated histories, and allegories

The changing fate of ancient myth from a reasonably reputable phenomenon, "a form of knowledge about the distant past"[1] to something spurious and suspicious, is in many respects an extraordinary occurrence. With regard to its former value in ancient Greece Burckhardt wrote,

> myth was a powerful force dominating Greek life and hovering over it all like a wonderful vision, close at hand. It illuminated the whole of the present for the Greeks, everywhere and until a very late date, as though it belonged to a quite recent past; and essentially it presented a sublime reflection of the perceptions and the life of the nation itself.[2]

Myths had dominated Greek life for very long but their relevance "in post-classical times was greatly diminished."[3] They ceased to offer explanations covering all aspects of human experience (man, society and reality) partly perhaps because of the fragmentation of Greco-Roman society.[4] Myth assumed various other functions, but somehow all seemed humbler and not as authoritative as its former functions. For instance, under the influence of the Sophists the pedagogical and instructive function of myths increased. This continues later on too, as for instance with the philosophies of the Stoics and the Cynics who shared "a taste for allegory and moral interpretations of myth."[5] These functions of myth posed less difficulties since the clear moral of the story would make "interpretation unnecessary."[6] Using myths in such a way was not new but now it seemed that myth had been reduced solely to the role of teacher and instructor.

To trace the various transformations of any historical concept or phenomenon is a very complex and delicate undertaking. One problem would be to see this concept or phenomenon as relatively stable

DOI: 10.4324/9781315387703-3

through time, having, that is, a certain identity that makes the tracing of the changes of this identity possible. In other words, are we certain that we always talk about the same thing and not something resembling it? Are historical concepts and phenomena relatively the same throughout history? Assuming that this identity does somehow exist, a second, and very much related, problem would be to be able to trace the various transformations of this concept or phenomenon, and define them in terms of decline or the opposite, a positive development of some sort. This is a central problem to history, as the issues of transformation and development are about historical process as such and thus inescapable. It may be argued that any reference to positive or negative development may invite ideas of progress or decline which are difficult to define historically, no matter how frequently they have been used to describe the historical process. With myths, however, a positive or negative development simply means that their various transformations either supported the initial historical character of myths or denied it. Denying it is seen as negative in so far as the loss of the historical character would also be a loss of the original and true purpose of myths.

The assumption in what follows in this section is that myths present a quite characteristic case where their identity has been retained to a remarkable degree throughout history (i.e., myth did not remain exactly the same thing but its relative identity made it a recognisable and a common point of reference) and their transformations can be more or less clearly marked as positive or, more frequently, negative. Both these things are quite unusual. Their identity because myth in a real sense stopped being a practice in almost all societies since antiquity or a bit later on. The transformations for the same reason, because they occurred to an old cultural practice, and as such one would expect that the forces responsible for the transformations would have had a reduced vitality or impact. Although, therefore, almost no post antiquity society produced myths in the way that ancient societies did, myth seems to be very much alive. It may be argued that there is a sense in which many societies kept producing new myths, albeit in most cases the new myths have rarely been the result of any real transformation of the initial concepts of myth. In that sense the new myths, if they exist at all, are not really myths but the result of some corruption in the understanding of the original concepts of myth. The persistence of myths indicates, however, that they have been of interest both because of their appeal and their interpretative difficulties, and also because of their ageless relevance as to what many people may find in them in terms of meaning and explanation. They have also elicited strong reactions and their transformations have been quite dramatic.

The story of the fate of myth is rather well documented. From late antiquity it followed a steady decline until the late seventeenth century. Then some more fruitful interpretations occurred with Vico and some of the Romantic thinkers, only to revert later on to fanciful and highly abstract theories which misunderstood or did not pay too much attention to the historical character of myths. One of the main purposes of this section is to offer some explanation as to why myths for centuries lost their historical relevance and became synonymous with false consciousness, lies, hidden meanings, bad science or even bad history. As we shall see the negative reputation that myths gradually acquired can be attributed both to inattentive and erroneous interpretations, and also to historical circumstances which purposely denigrated myths. Erroneous interpretations have been, and in some respects still are, the result of various factors, including the difficulties myths present to anyone who wishes to understand them. Such interpretations would not necessarily imply any hostility towards them. The deliberate denigration of myth, however, attempted to weaken any metaphysical claim that myth had brought forward, at a time when grand metaphysical schemes were regarded with suspicion as conceptual errors.

There are two main groups of explanations. The first will be considered in conjunction with R.G. Collingwood's criticisms. Collingwood had produced an unfinished study in fairy tales, in which he saw these tales as having a mythical core. Unravelling the historical potential of this material Collingwood had something to say about the methodologies of three schools that had attempted to interpret this material. We will look into this in the next section. For now it would suffice to add that this first group of explanations, although most certainly historical in some respects, somehow transcends historical periods and contingencies as such, because its motivation can not be found in any combination of historical factors. It is more like a tendency, a peculiar or intrinsic feature of thought. It manifests itself in various periods under different pretences whose common element is the aspiration to offer an abstract account of the phenomena under consideration, including myths. It offers a highly speculative framework as it examines its subject matter, any subject matter, partially or completely detached from its original context and under mysterious categories that allegedly the subject matter possesses but does not really and clearly exhibit. It is again a game of finding those hidden meanings and the scholar, instead of bringing a historical attitude to the enquiry, becomes a decipherer of those meanings. Culture in general was treated in such a fashion, but the cryptic quality of myths has encouraged this tendency even further and myths have often been the field where those interpretations collided with imaginary problems.

The second group deals with the historical vicissitudes which resulted in the various transmutations of myths. These changes are explicable as mere incidents in the historical process. Euhemerism and the vast range of allegorical interpretations fall into this category. In Euhemerism, for instance, the historicity of myths loses its real value as we are taken to a realm where historical accuracy seems even less plausible than some excesses of myth itself. Euhemerus of Messene was a Greek historian and mythographer who in his *Sacred Document* written around 300 B.C. talked about gods who once upon a time were men and women whose various real deeds and identity had been distorted by later layers of fanciful and untrue features. This is a story whose validity Euhemerus believed had demonstrated by historical research. His story was based on an inscription he had found in the temple of Zeus in Panchaea, an imaginary island in the Indian Ocean, an inscription which revealed the history of the gods since Uranus, a history of great, mortal, rulers.[7] Those mortal people, "after dying normal deaths, had been buried in places that [Euhemerus] was able to point out."[8] Euhemerism was an interpretative school already present in antiquity, which continued in the Middle Ages and almost until Vico's time any historical interpretation of myths would fall under the name of Euhemerism. It is not quite clear why Euhemerism is even considered a historical interpretation and not a rationalistic one, explaining the origins of gods and perhaps even religion in a way that may be conceived as atheistic. The ancients themselves certainly did consider it as such, its influence as an explanation of the origins of the gods was not great, and writers such as Cicero and Plutarch "denied and condemned it as impious and absurd."[9] Not surprisingly Euhemerism's implications did not go unnoticed by the early Christian fathers. They detected in this a great opportunity to direct against their pagan antagonists the charge that they worship gods who were merely human beings. It is not perfectly clear if Euhemerus himself had any intention to undermine gods or religion, but his ideas were indeed used to attack pagan, religious beliefs. It was, in fact, a potent weapon in "the centuries-long struggle of the Church against the myths of the pagan gods."[10] Euhemerism came also to exemplify the concept of dubious mythical history and significantly diminished the historical credibility of myths.

The second group of explanations (myths changing due to historical vicissitudes) also includes changes which may be explicable not as historical incidents or accidents, but as intentional responses to modes of thinking which, at some point, happened to be out of sympathy with the prevailing cultural and intellectual moods. These changes have more political or politicised motives. To the extent that such motivation is usually polemical, their responses may be disingenuous, factually inaccurate, exaggerated or entirely invented. An illuminating example of this tendency to produce arguments with dubious quality can be found in Voltaire.

With Voltaire his anti-religious, especially anti-Christian, attitude, combined with his belief in historical progress and his preference for philosophical history, guaranteed from the outset that any attempt at writing history would have had serious problems to overcome with regard to proper historical method. As Frederick Copleston had pointed out, when Voltaire "talks about the need for writing history in a philosophical spirit, he is referring to the need for excluding legends and fairy-stories. ... Quite apart from the fact that a study of such legends, and even of the oracles of Delphi can be, as Vico saw but Voltaire did not, of great use to the serious historian, the remedy for uncertain and fabulous history is patient research."[11] This patient, principled and disinterested historical research Voltaire was not prepared to undertake for, among other things, it would verify the uncomfortable fact that the entire structure of ancient European societies was substantially religious and remained so for centuries. Myth was supporting that structure, it was a vital element in those early religions. A proper historical research would have to engage with myths and try to understand what they meant for those ancient people. It would also require to recover the religious elements and meaning embedded in those myths and face a world where the religious sentiment animated all aspects of life and gave answers to practical and metaphysical concerns alike. This was something that most thinkers of the Enlightenment were not prepared to do, to engage sympathetically with ancient religions and myths. Branding entire historical periods as irrational and unenlightened would provide enough justification to ignore their importance, and the difficult task of understanding and explaining them would become unnecessary. Voltaire, thus, involved myths in the general attack on religion. From strange and unverifiable assertions, such as that myths were "false statements about reality invented by wicked priests to bamboozle and acquire power over the masses",[12] to attacking myths in order to defend Deism, Voltaire's interpretation of myths, history and the past is not so much speculative and selective as invented. He "rewrites the past so that the Bible and Greece play only minor roles" and "rejects myth as patent superstition and historical distortion."[13] With ancient Greece, Christianity and the Middle Ages sorted, Voltaire turned his attention to the East for something more constructive. Here too his prejudices and the speculative character of his views on history distort the historical record in order to support his grand synthesis. But the distortion has now been inverted and in the benign East even religion has behaved differently as Voltaire found out:

> "tell me if there be any other people than the Christians and the Jews, whom zeal and religion, unhappily turned into fanaticism, have prompted to so many horrible cruelties?"
>
> "Yes," said he; "the Mahometans have been stained by the same inhuman acts, but rarely; ... As for other nations, not one of them, since the beginning of the world, has ever made a purely religious war."[14]

In this imaginary dialogue with "one of those genii who fill the spaces between worlds,"[15] it is Voltaire asking the questions and Voltaire who provides the answers: any historical evidence comes largely from his own personal opinions and its value as evidence diminishes rather quickly.

Despite, or perhaps because of, its deistic aspirations the Enlightenment is commonly and justifiably viewed as "a revolt not only against the power of institutional religion but against religion as such."[16] Voltaire and the deists had, however, failed to see that mythology and ancient religions, naïve as they may have been in proper religious terms, offered a more comprehensive answer than Deism to the vexing questions of reality, creation and the cosmos. When the old and traditional points of reference (faith, revelation, etc.) have been removed from religion, what remains is a shifting spirituality unattached to formal structures, tenets and participation. This spirituality begins vaguely animated by the awareness that there is something barely comprehensible that demands clarification. But it moves very little from there. It remains essentially a subjective, personal, and lonely quest, with reason alone providing more and more opportunities to revert to scepticism and rejection. In this sense it remains doubtful whether it is at all possible to study myths from a secular, or semi-secular, point of view. For it may be argued that every explanatory attempt that originates from a secular source will not be able to grasp all the nuances and the world view of a religiously leaning society, the environment which supported the creation and development of myths. Myth was one of the things that gave expression to this world view, expressing it in historical form.

Myth, history and religion were, thus, linked in ways that any secular and rationalistic understanding would find a priori questionable. The rejection of myths by the rationalism of the Enlightenment may be seen in this wider context of the advancing tendencies of secularism and the attack on religion. It was assisted in part by the ethnological and anthropological material amassed during the previous centuries, creating an interesting, although fallacious, logic through associating present-day savages with ancient cultures and dismissing them both as primitive and irrational. Thus the absurdity of religions and myths was thought to have been established. It was perhaps one of the first instances that the accusation of irrationalism was used in such a way against cultural manifestations. It was an odd and rather weak response but one that was to become quite influential in years to come. It was often unclear on what basis the charge of irrationality was being made, the argument contained a certain circularity, and there was almost an unwillingness to engage genuinely with the subject matter in question. It also contained elements that were to become familiar, the employment of a-historical, conceptual categories with no definite and clear content. The term irrational, for example, is too broad and vague enough to be able to accommodate equally broad and vague interpretations. Progressively irrationalism would be intricately connected with views which were taken to indicate an opposition to the scientific spirit. Every form, that is, of thought which is not compatible with certain ideas of science as posited, postulated and understood during different stages of its development. The real issue, therefore, was not the conflict between science and other forms of knowledge and explanation. It was, and in many ways it remains so, the struggle for ultimate answers between not so much fields of knowledge but modes of interpretation, one of which appears to be a *type* of science allegedly expressing the only way that science is possible. Collingwood in his *An Essay on Metaphysics* almost reversed this idea, making science as a whole dependent on religious foundations:

> The guardianship of the European 'scientific frame of mind' is vested in the religious institutions of European civilization. In any civilization it is man's religious institutions that refresh in him from time to time the will (for it is a matter of will, though not a matter of choice) to retain the presuppositions by whose aid he reduces such experience as he enjoys to such science as he can compass; and it is by dint of these same religious institutions that he transmits the same presuppositions to his children. For if science is 'experience' interpreted in the light of our general

convictions as to the nature of the world, religion is what expresses these convictions in themselves and for their own sake and hands them on from generation to generation.[17]

The scientific frame of mind is something quite important and much wider than just science, especially a purely materialistic science without noticeable ethical and transcendental connections. The latter would undermine and render meaningless many areas of culture and civilisation, including any genuine historical enquiry. As we shall see in the following section, Collingwood described aptly this particular attitude and its fallacies.

Notes

1 Graf, *Greek Mythology*, 178.
2 Burckhardt, *Greeks and Greek Civilization*, 22-3.
3 Graf, *Greek Mythology*, 178.
4 Ibid.
5 Flacelière, *Literary History of Greece*, 334.
6 Graf, *Greek Mythology*, 183.
7 Ibid., 192.
8 Cooke, "Euhemerism," 397.
9 Ibid., 396-7.
10 Taylor Stevenson, *History as Myth*, 63.
11 Copleston, *History of Philosophy*, 166-7.
12 Berlin, *Vico and Herder*, 193.
13 Feldman and Richardson, *Rise of Modern Mythology*, 151.
14 From "Philosophical Dictionary. On Religion", quoted in ibid., 154.
15 Ibid., 153.
16 Collingwood, *Idea of History*, 76.
17 Collingwood, *An Essay on Metaphysics*, 198. For Collingwood's general argument of religion as the absolute presupposition of science see mainly ibid., 185-227.

References

Berlin, Isaiah. *Vico and Herder. Two Studies in the History of Ideas*. London: The Hogarth Press, 1976.
Burckhardt, Jacob. *The Greeks and Greek Civilization*. Edited by Oswyn Murray, translated by Sheila Stern. New York: St Martin's Press, 1998.
Collingwood, Robin George. *An Essay on Metaphysics*. Oxford: Oxford Clarendon Press, 1940 (Revised Edition with an introduction and additional material edited by Rex Martin, 1998).
Collingwood, Robin George. *The Idea of History*. Oxford: Oxford University Press, 1946 (Revised edition with Lectures 1926-1928, edited with an introduction by Jan van der Dussen, Oxford: Oxford University Press, 1994).

Cooke, John Daniel. "Euhemerism: A Mediaeval Interpretation of Classical Paganism." *Speculum* 2, no. 4 (October 1927): 396–410.

Copleston, Frederick. *A History of Philosophy*, Vol. VI. *Wolff to Kant.* London: Burns and Oates Ltd, 1968.

Feldman, Burton, and Richardson, Robert D. *The Rise of Modern Mythology, 1680-1860.* Bloomington: Indiana University Press, 1972.

Flacelière, Robert. *A Literary History of Greece*, Translated by Douglas Garman. London: Elek Books Ltd, 1964.

Graf, Fritz. *Greek Mythology. An Introduction*, Translated by Thomas Marier. Baltimore and London: The John Hopkins University Press, 1993.

Taylor Stevenson, William. *History as Myth. The Import for Contemporary Theology.* New York: The Seabury Press, 1969.

3 The significance of method: R.G. Collingwood and fairy tales as myths

A very little known aspect of the story of the renewed historical interest in myths was R.G. Collingwood's contribution.[1] In the second half of the 1930s Collingwood was already an established authority of Roman Britain and a philosopher of some repute, having being elected in 1935 to the Waynflete Chair of Metaphysical Philosophy at Oxford. In 1936, or shortly after and certainly before 1938,[2] he devoted time to the examination of fairy tales. Unpublished until relatively recently, and almost entirely unknown beyond specialist scholarship, Collingwood's study provides an interesting alternative during a period where new challenges, methodological anomalies, and a-historical approaches besieged the examination of myths. Although mainly about fairy tales, and in particular fairy tales found in the British Isles, Collingwood thought that the themes found in those tales can be regarded as myths and could be used as historical evidence if properly approached and interpreted. His study remained unfinished but it was a serious undertaking[3] and quite evident that he intended to produce a substantial, book length, treatment of the topic. As to why his task remained incomplete we can only speculate.[4] In this projected book Collingwood returned, in a somehow modified way, to familiar themes which had frequently preoccupied him in the past. The choice of the subject matter is certainly uncommon. Uncommon even for Collingwood's historical proclivities, his wide ranging interests, and at times unfashionable and unconventional philosophical tastes. Adding also his uncommonly heavy work load, his teaching and archaeological commitments, and his always precarious, and by now gradually failing, health, the choice to spend time on a topic with a distinct unphilosophical reputation raises the question as to how he conceived his priorities during the late 1930s.[5]

One reason might have been that this specific study could allow Collingwood to explore some aspects of religion. Religion had always been an area of importance for Collingwood. His first major book in

DOI: 10.4324/9781315387703-4

1916 was a study of religion and philosophy whose aim was "to treat the Christian creed not as dogma but as a critical solution of a philosophical problem."[6] Collingwood approached Christianity as a philosophy, and the Christian doctrines as "aspects of a single idea which, according to the language in which it is expressed, may be called a metaphysic, an ethic, or a theology."[7] Elsewhere religion was conceived as the "vital warmth at the heart of a civilization ... the passion which inspires a society to persevere in a certain way of life and to obey the rules which define it."[8] It was the diminishing religious energy, the decline of Christianity in several European countries, that Collingwood considered the main reason for civilisation's dire condition. The opportunity to study myths in order to find more about the origins of European religion and the structure of the early European societies was, for a historically minded person like Collingwood, a fascinating prospect.

His study also offers an interesting account of methodological problems by examining how substantially different were the result of various interpretative attempts to study this material. This for Collingwood indicated a problem, one found throughout his writings: to forget that the study of nature and the study of human affairs ought to be conducted by different methods. To confuse those two enterprises by using the same method for both is a serious mistake. Collingwood's study delved into the strange world of folklore, fairy tales, myths, primitive life, magic, taboo, totemism, etc. and tried to show how less mysterious all these can be when the method of history is operative.

The historical character of fairy tales

Collingwood begins his study with the simple idea that everything "men have made can be used as evidence for their history; but in order so to use it, we must find out how to interpret it."[9] Thus he quickly establishes two main considerations, the historical usefulness of even the most humble and seemingly trivial aspects of human activities, and the importance of method. His choice is one of those less celebrated aspects as he intends to suggest "how fairy tales may be used as historical evidence."[10] Collingwood regarded fairy tales as traditional stories, handed down from the past by oral transmission, and by traditional stories he meant that they "constitute a social institution carefully preserved by the people."[11] Thus as a vital institution those stories may be kept alive for a very long time, altered and modified to reflect the changes in society, and when ultimately come down to us we may have good reason to believe that "certain themes embedded in them are several thousand years old."[12] Despite the changes and modifications that these stories underwent, a certain continuity may have been preserved in them. Collingwood saw fairy tales as relics of customs and beliefs and he suggested that by stripping off the various layers of their subsequent history we would find evidence of their earlier stages. This is certainly a very ambitious plan and requires considerable historical skill. Collingwood recognises the various difficulties of provenance, diffusion etc.[13] He maintains that it is not an insurmountable problem because cultural borrowings indicate that "whatever was borrowed was something capable of incorporation in the existing culture of the borrowers."[14] Thus even if a tale originated elsewhere and was subsequently borrowed by a different cultural environment, the themes embedded in the tale will be able to give us historical information about that second culture, in so far as the tale was put into a different use from that culture. Based on this reasoning Collingwood argued that in order to use those tales as historical evidence we would need to accept two principles "that the themes found in fairy tales are organically connected with the customs and beliefs of the people who originated them, and that customs and beliefs are things which have a history."[15] Collingwood historicises the tales, we would need to know their specific context and their historical provenance in order to be able to say something about them. Abstract psychological assumptions claiming that fairy tale themes are connected with the unconscious and thus symbolise "inward dramas that go on everywhere and always in the human mind"[16] are to be discounted. If this were true the fairy stories could not be used as historical evidence. At most they could give us a description of people in general but not of specific people and their history. Universal psychological symbols, if they exist at all, are not bound by specific historical circumstances and "the same theme might spring up spontaneously in any part of the world at any date."[17] The specific context would be irrelevant, just the accidental geographical and chronological coordinates of another instance confirming some universal human tendency.

Collingwood argued that the way he proposed to study fairy tales was rather unlike previous attempts, although those tales "have been actively and profitably studied for more than a hundred years."[18] He does not mention it but fairy tales as historically valuable was an idea also put forward by John Ruskin who, complaining about various attempts to moralise fairy tales, asserted that, the effect of the endeavour to make stories moral upon the literary merit of the work itself, is as harmful as the motive of the effort is false. For every fairy tale worth recording at all is the remnant of a tradition possessing true historical value; – historical, at least, in so far as it has naturally arisen out of the mind of a people under special circumstances, and risen not without meaning, nor removed altogether from their sphere of religious faith.[19]

Any attempt to moralise those tales would mean to solidify some of their features into idealised forms instead of seeing them as customs, beliefs, modes of behaviour and so forth, of the societies who invented them. In other words seeing them as historical evidence which could augment human self knowledge. Interestingly Ruskin also alluded to the religious element of those tales, a feature perhaps indicative of their great antiquity and of the basic structure of those societies.

Collingwood did not mention Ruskin but he did discuss three other interpretative attempts. His terminology and periodisation are idiosyncratic but rather easily understood. The first he calls the German philological school, dated roughly 1810–70, and examined the ideas of brothers Grimm and of Max Müller. The second is that of the anthropological folklorists or functional anthropologists, dated 1870–1910, and he focused on the work of Edward Burnett Tylor and of Sir James George Frazer. The third is the psychological school, dated 1900–20, represented by Sigmund Freud and Carl Jung. Collingwood limited himself to these schools as he thought that various promising developments during his lifetime were not as yet ready for proper historical evaluation.

The connection with myths is established early on since the German philological school, according to Collingwood, considered fairy tales "as 'myths' describing natural phenomena in poetic or metaphorical language."[20] This was mainly Müller's idea. Through postulating a common Aryan identity a common mythological tradition became possible. Müller concluded that ancient myths were a process of symbolism, a poetic way to describe "the events attending the sun's daily path through the sky: the dawn, the high noon, sunset, and night."[21] Collingwood believed that the problem was not so much that Müller was willing to see in every story such sun-myths, but the way he treats his evidence, emphasising that which can be made to fit his theory, ignoring everything else. What is achieved by this method is that the very essence of mythology comes into question, "why mythology should exist at all."[22] If every instance of a story examined by Müller reveals a sun-myth told in a symbolic, metaphorical way,

Collingwood wonders why this should be the case. For one might expect that this alleged fascination of the primitive Aryan people with the sun's daily cycle could be described "in plain Aryan" rather than being wrapped up "in this maze of riddles."[23] Müller's own explanation is his well known 'disease of language' theory. He postulated a mythological age which had succeeded the origins of language, and during that age irrationality and even temporary insanity disturbed the usual thought processes and affected language too. Mythology was the confused product of this ailing language. Müller's explanation was not based on any available historical evidence. It was invented in order to explain his own theory of mythology, which after constructing had found difficult to believe. However erroneous his theory may have been, it must have been a creation of considerable effort, decoding and interpreting those elaborate Aryan stories. Even if those Aryan people had wished to hide their ideas behind riddles, they had done it convincingly. Their stories were not ravings, there was a rather remarkable lucidity in the way their alleged insanity manifested itself. To take all these into account and still draw the conclusion that this whole affair was predicated on insanity and linguistic confusion, was what made Collingwood ask if this could not be "a symbolic picture of the unreason at work" in Müller himself. But Müller was not unreasonable, his was a case where the problem of method becomes evident. Irrationality comes to assist as an invented category to explain things that appear to him inexplicable otherwise. But it is a category selectively and unfairly used: up to a point the primitive Aryans seemed rational enough to provide him with material that he wanted to understand further. But they become irrational of no fault of their own, after all they did not interpret that material. Effectively Müller accuses them of being confused for something of his own making. His belief that his theory must be correct and that the ancient people must have been confused and irrational epitomises the lack of historical spirit in approaching a historical problem.

Tylor, according to Collingwood, was one of the main initiators of the anthropological school and someone who understood the primitive mind reasonably well. Tylor also sees fairy tales as myths and classified them into groups of natural phenomena: earth, sky, sun, moon, rainbow etc.[24] Thus although, unlike Müller, he does not see myths as linguistic accidents his explanation as to their function is similar since they imaginatively describe natural phenomena, "a kind of poetic science of nature."[25] Tylor believes that this poetical or imaginative description is the result of seeing natural forces as persons, a tendency or even a fundamental feature of the primitive mind to give a human like quality to everything. This all encompassing anthropomorphism is his theory of animism. So here again we have a theory explaining another theory which was strange to begin with, namely that people use elaborate stories to describe natural phenomena, embellishing and complicating something that could have been expressed in simpler language. It seems, therefore, that Tylor's theory of animism served the same purpose as Müller's theory of language. In Collingwood's evaluation Tylor's study of mythology did not achieve definite results but made possible for others to follow some of the consequences of his doctrine of survivals. The idea, that is, that certain things that appear to us now strange survive from an earlier culture whose context will help us understand the meaning of these survivals. This gradually led to the realisation that certain classes of myths or fairy tales were not poetic, imaginative, or metaphorical descriptions of natural phenomena, but literal accounts of rituals.[26] Thus the entire idea of myth seemed to change, from a metaphor for natural phenomena became part, a vital ingredient, of a cultural custom. These new anthropological ideas were taken up and steadily produced some fruitful results and a different outlook. Individual cultures were viewed as a single whole "in which every element is connected with every other."[27] This was most certainly a romantic contribution, the notion of cultures as interconnected, interdependent systems. Thus myths were seeing not as irrational expressions of 'primitive' or 'savage' people but as important aspects of their lives. The 'primitive' life itself began to make more sense, as embedding the actions of people who were quite practical, systematic, and logical. It also became increasingly clear that myth and ritual were intimately connected and myth was not just a subsequent invention to explain the ritual, the idea of the aetiological myth had to be abandoned. Instead it was understood that "myth and ritual were not related as consequence to antecedent, but were coexistent parts of a single indivisible whole."[28] The work, however, of the anthropological school was, according to Collingwood, partly successful. By examining the work of James Frazer, Collingwood concluded that Frazer's principles were in various ways defective.[29] One problem, for instance, was that he attempted to explain certain myths (and customs in general) by referring to other myths found in different cultures and thus creating a theory based on tenuous similarities but not supported by the available evidence. Also, Collingwood believed that Frazer approached his subject matter naturalistically, as an external spectacle, and not historically, as an experience with which he could sympathise by penetrating the thoughts of his fellow-men.

Lastly Collingwood considered the psychological theories by focusing on Freud and Jung.[30] As anthropology had made clear that fairy tales and myths should be examined in conjunction with the entire culture in which they arise, Collingwood considered the psychological theories as offering general insights into culture. On the whole he found those insights disappointing. With Freud the phenomena of 'primitive' life and culture would become manifestations of mental derangement, especially neurosis. Freud being a specialist in mental disease and using the complicate web of his own theories about repression, Oedipus complex, sexual urges and the like, constructed an image of the 'savage' as hopelessly confused and a compulsive neurotic. Inspired by him there was something like "a Freudian school of folklore"[31] where the study of myths and fairy tales turned into a pasttime of finding their hidden sexual symbolisms. Every myth became a sexual symbol, not unlike the formula of Müller where every story was a sun-myth. With Jung myths again become symbolic ways of expressing what is "in the 'mind' of the 'folk'."[32] Instead of natural phenomena alone, now they also express the intimate wishes of the folk-mind. Myths, for Jung, are a relic of a myth making era, "an age of corporate childhood"[33] and they are also somehow connected with dreams, where the various distinctions between corporate and individual mind are blurred to sustain similarities between the activities of myths and dreams. Those fictitious origins of myths and dreams, attributed to an imaginary period of the infancy of people, are further combined with the idea of the existence of a vital impulse or energy, libido in Jung's terminology. Now every story and every myth becomes not a sun symbol or a sex symbol but a libido symbol, where libido essentially symbolises power. This is so generic and broad that to call something a power symbol "is to call it nothing at all."[34]

The value of method

Collingwood maintained that all three schools made the same mistake: using naturalistic methods to deal with a problem which is historical in nature.[35] Given that any civilisation is the product of some sort of development, where a more advanced civilisation comes out of a more primitive one, the anthropologist finds himself almost in a living past, and must recognise in the 'savage' he studies something that he also possesses, "a savage within him, in the special sense in which any historical present contains within itself its own past."[36] Anthropology, therefore, becomes "a special case of the problem of self-knowledge"[37] For Collingwood, man can not be studied as an external, observable phenomenon, but as something familiar that every man possesses within him, and "what he finds when he looks within him is his own history."[38] The only way that this study is possible is by employing the methods of history so that "man's thought and actions can become the object of human knowledge."[39] The methodological difference between history and natural science is not only how the object of the enquiry is perceived – as an external phenomenon to be observed and classified, or as some internal truth to be understood. A phenomenon for natural science is not interesting as such but only as an instance in order to be able to draw more general conclusions. The quest for uniformity and for finding similarities is overwhelming. Thus when the naturalistic method is extended beyond its legitimate boundaries there is a tendency to ignore details and variations, over-emphasise similarities and thus "reduce to a spurious uniformity things which may well be essentially different."[40] History, on the other hand, being concerned with the individual and not the general, sees details, variances, and differences as essential, each case being of unique interest and not an instance of some future generalisation. According to Collingwood, suppressing, ignoring or arbitrarily distinguishing between important and unimportant details means that the evidence is used disingenuously and the result is not historical knowledge but the construction of images of the past (or, in the case of anthropology, of the primitive cultures under study) according to the desires of the would-be historian.[41] This is an appropriate point, for the various images of the past we possess are often emotionally coloured. Overly positive images commonly evoke lost paradises and golden ages and lament for their loss and for our current degradation. Collingwood's examples, from the three schools he examined, had created the opposite image, one of past folly, insanity and neurosis. Both images warp the past and corrupt our opportunities to achieve self-knowledge through history.

In summary, Collingwood thought that a naturalistic method would do two things if used to examine historical problems: first, it would treat details selectively, using only those deemed right for generalisation purposes; secondly this unprincipled selectivity leads to results not based on evidence but on preconceived ideas guided by emotional predilections and desires. In order to avoid those dangers Collingwood proposes two principles of sound historical method. Before examining these two principles it is worth clarifying a point. Collingwood had always been very interested in matters of method. However he never expounded a detailed methodology specifically for history, nor for that matter a definite theory of history. His ideas on these issues can be reconstructed by various references in his writings[42] but they are still a matter of considerable discussion among specialist scholars. Some of Collingwood's methodological ideas have clearer philosophical undertones attempting, among other things, to describe how historical knowledge becomes possible. Re-enactment is one such idea and it is also present in his fairy tales study, although not extensively discussed, and only once or twice mentioned by that name (recreation and reconstruction are also used, possibly having the same meaning as re-enactment).[43] As opposed to Collingwood's more philosophical ideas on method, the two principles in the fairy tales study seem to be designed to offer more help in the actual historical practice. They also seem more appropriate for a work which was meant, at least in part, as a conventional historical study, an exploration of the origins of European religion and society. In what follows the emphasis will be on those two principles.

The first principle is Spinoza's altered maxim "neither to condemn nor to deride the feelings and actions of men, but to understand them."[44] This is clearly not a philosophical doctrine about how historical knowledge is possible but a common sense approach, that the thoughts and actions of people are intelligible, no matter how unfamiliar, perplexing, and strange they may appear to us. It is exactly because there are so many perplexing instances of human behaviour that the attitude of the student of it should be open to the possibility of encountering an unusual or unheard of action, custom or belief and be prepared to deal with it. It would, thus, be preferable to begin with a vocabulary that contains no terms of contempt, ridicule or disparagement and with the assumption that human behaviour is always explainable.[45] This does not imply that human behaviour is always successful or does not exemplify folly. But even these should be explainable as instances of attempts that went wrong and thus be able to give a reason as to why this has happened. To be able to say that failures occur not because people "are fools in general ... [but] because they are a special kind of fool."[46] Such broad understanding is certainly challenging for it requires the suspension of our current set of beliefs and the expansion of our view in good faith that other sets of beliefs may also make sense. To be able to do so we need to understand ourselves historically, because "history is man's knowledge of man ... [and] demands, or rather brings about, a peculiar intimacy in the relation between knower and known."[47] Collingwood maintained that any historian in order to understand a thought must think "it over again for himself" and if there is "any type of thinking which for any reason he is unable to do for himself, he cannot thus rethink it and cannot understand it historically."[48] A historian must have "inner experience of [the] thought-forms"[49] he is trying to rethink and understand. Now, admittedly, any historian's personal experience is rather limited and it is very likely that he may not have had actual experience of very many things he is trying to study and understand. It is conceivable that 'experience' and 'thought-forms' are concepts that refer to something wider than a person's own experience. In those concepts we may recognise ourselves, through different or past cultures, as those potentialities which did not materialise for us but they might as well have been our own ways. There is nothing particularly odd in considering experience as something that includes possibilities and potentialities of some sort, otherwise thinking, communication, and understanding would be much more restricted activities than they are. This is the complex vision and burden of history with dissimilar, unequal, and even antithetical and incompatible perspectives, but all judgements of a common human fate.

The second principle is Bishop Butler's adjusted maxim that "every thing is what it is, and not another thing."[50] This for Collingwood means to realise that the study is historical and not naturalistic and that facts, details, peculiarities and distinctions are important and not mere instances or unimportant features which encumber the overall picture. Any historical picture is composed of all those details and distinguishing finely is what makes each historical period different from all others. It is precisely when we suppress the details and ignore the differences that some alleged confusion is detected in primitive societies, where one thing was erroneously identified with another. Collingwood mentions three such examples of confusion: the identification of the priest-king with the god; the relation between the god and "the things in which or through which he works"; and the confusion between "the different ways in which the same power works."[51] Collingwood analyses these examples by using counter examples from modern life to demonstrate that the gap between different modes of thinking has often unexpected similarities. The first example has been seen as an indication of irrational thinking, identifying a human being with god. But this, Collingwood argues, is only the dramatic form that a fertility ritual takes, where the priest-king impersonates the god and remains in this role for the rest of his life, for his "whole life is a sacred ritual."[52] This does not mean that his people are not able to distinguish between the human person of the priest-king and his other 'persona' when impersonating the god. In the second example while a man may, for instance, regard "as divine the power in his stone axe which enables it to cut down trees", he does not mistake the stone of the axe for a god, and is able to distinguish between the material object and its physical body from the powers he thinks may reside in it.[53] The last example is the idea of the waste land, the belief that "the king's ill-health causes the land to become waste".[54] Collingwood argues that in order to understand this connection properly we need to understand the structure of those primitive, agricultural societies. The myth of the waste land is "a function of agricultural ritual, and when regarded in its proper social setting is seen to be no idle superstition but a shrewd observation of important facts."[55] If we want, therefore, to interpret these things we would need to reconstruct the social structure of those societies which produced them and the only way to do so is by using the right method: a historical method based only on available evidence and factual detail and not on abstractions and generalisations.[56]

How this method would have been applied was meant to be Collingwood's concluding part of his book. The initial plan was to study certain classes of themes in fairy tales found in the British Isles[57] but it remained incomplete. Only several variants of the *Cinderella* story were in the end examined. Although the treatment is relatively lengthy it is mainly the descriptive and the classificatory sections that occupy most of it, the interpretation is only a smaller fragment.[58] From this fragment we see that Collingwood tried to establish that the European variants of the *Cinderella* story had absorbed ideas current in Europe between the Middle Ages – tenth century or so – and the seventeenth century. These ideas were "strongly enough held to in-fluence the structure of stories passing from mouth to mouth and to impose upon them a significance which they did not originally pos-sess."[59] The most important such idea was the identity of the mother with a helpful animal and what this idea further implies. Namely that a human being may be an animal and an animal a human being, and as such an animal that protects and guides its own human kinship group, and also that those human beings protected by the helpful animal are also animals of the same species.[60] Collingwood regards that where the two ideas are found together, the helpful animal and the belief that humans can become animals, there exists a very strong indications of totemism. Where, that is, "a certain group of persons related by blood at once regard animals of a certain kind as their natural hereditary friends, and also regard themselves as members of that animal species and vice versa."[61] Collingwood seems quite aware of the pitfalls of the term totemism, its many meanings and also of the fact that even in his days the term was losing its former popularity. But he is quite con-vinced by the available evidence that during the Middle Ages, when the European version of the *Cinderella* stories got crystallised, there were "relics of totemistic beliefs and of magical practices based on them, garbled no doubt, but recognizable, existing in most parts of Europe and specially in the east, north, and north-west."[62] His is not, however, a complete theory of totemism but just a prolegomenon to such study, a "rough description of the motives [motifs] underlying any totemistic religion and social order."[63] This religion was for Collingwood primarily associated with hunting and food gathering societies and not agricultural civilisations, although such beliefs survived, for various reasons, the adoption of agricultural practices.[64] Collingwood believed that the great age of totemism in Europe must have been the Palaeolithic period. Subsequently there must have been a series of survivals of totemistic beliefs and practices, from the Neolithic and the Bronze Age down to the Middle Ages, progressively more and more distorted and fragmentary, and appearing as elements of popular superstitions. In the Middle Ages they would have taken the form of relics of pagan customs, mixed with other pagan relics from agricultural religions.

This is in effect where Collingwood's interpretation breaks off and it is rather difficult to see the complete picture he was trying to recreate. It is not, for instance, quite clear what forms the relics of totemistic beliefs took with every new survival and how this process was recorded in order to be able to be traced and used as historical evidence; or why some of these ideas were absorbed by fairy tales, why would this incorporation have occurred at all. Collingwood did suggest, however, that a long oral tradition may have been indeed the case, and that in theory we should not doubt that it is possible that "a story collected in the nineteenth century may have been continuously told ever since the Bronze Age or even the Neolithic."[65] He was quite confident that it was indeed feasible to extract historical information from this complex material. This material comes from the past through various transformations, so it retains certain information about its origins. It contains relics of beliefs, customs, rituals, and practices that may help us reconstruct the social structure of ancient societies. It is also, broadly speaking, mythical material. Mythical in the sense that its themes are embedded in and conveyed through stories. These stories are not conventional historical narratives because they are told in a way ostensibly cryptic and fantastical, and are full of elements that would be regarded as non-historical accretions borrowed from legends and superstitions. It was perhaps this unconventional character of those stories that makes them, or should make them, a perfect subject matter for the historian. From his own historical and archaeological practice Collingwood had realised that obscure areas appealed to him because:

Their obscurity is a challenge; you have to invent new methods for studying them, and then you will probably find that the cause of their obscurity is some defect in the methods hitherto used. When these defects have been removed, it will be possible to revise the generally accepted opinions about other, more familiar, subjects, and to correct the errors with which those opinions are perhaps infected.[66]

The same he thought about Vico who had chosen to study the history of remote antiquity and also difficult aspects of it such as mythology, etymology and legend:

He studied distant and obscure periods precisely because they were distant and obscure; for his real interest was in historical method, and, according as the sources are scanty and dubious and the subject-matter strange and hard to understand, the importance of sound method becomes plain.[67]

Methodology was the key for Collingwood. In *The New Leviathan* he had described the dangers of using the wrong method in terms evocative of a fairy tale story:

2.72. If the wretched horse called Mental Science has stuck you in mid-stream you can flog him, or you can coax him, or you can get out and lead him; or you can drown, as better men than you have drowned before.

2.73. But you must not swap him even for the infinitely superior horse called Natural Science.

2.74. For this is a magical journey, and if you do that the river will vanish and you will find yourself back where you started.[68]

It was against the methodological defects of the three schools he analysed that the primacy of the historical method should be established. And through it fairy tales and myths become now legitimate and useful forms of human activity, offering invaluable insights into the ancient beliefs and religions of Europe.

Notes

1 For some general background of Collingwood's study see the introductions by the three editors: Smallwood, *Philosophy of Enchantment*, xxiii-lv; James, *Philosophy of Enchantment*, lvi-xci; Boucher, *Philosophy of Enchantment*, xcii-cxix.

2 The fairy tales writings are undated but from various internal elements and some indicative historical details from Collingwood's career the date of composition was between 1936 and 1938.

3 The seriousness of this endeavour is observed by all Collingwood's commentators, who agree that the folklore writings can, among other things, be considered as an answer to his grave concerns for a civilisation in crisis.

4 There is no definite answer as to why Collingwood did not finish the book on fairy tales. Smallwood argued that Collingwood "set them aside unpublished partly through illness, and perhaps to focus more completely on *The Principles of Art*" (Smallwood, *Philosophy of Enchantment*, xxxii). Both reasons, however, seem uncharacteristic of Collingwood's habits. For one he had no difficulty working on several projects simultaneously, quite capable of concentrating and producing work very quickly. On the other hand his fragile health had always been an issue since his student days where his health problems had begun, possibly as a result of his insomnia. Collingwood's output however hardly diminished even by the onset of his more serious illness. His inability and reluctance to conform to a less rigorous working routine, as instructed by his doctors, was perhaps what precipitated his passing. It is also quite evident that his illness did not have any significant effect upon the quality of his writings. All these points had been described by Collingwood himself: "Whether luckily or unluckily, I have never known any illness interfere with my power of thinking and writing, or with the quality of what I think and write. When I am unwell, I have only to begin work on some piece of philosophical writing, and all my ailments are forgotten until I leave off." (Collingwood, *Autobiography*, 117)

5 Some other explanations as to why Collingwood was interested in those stories emphasise the "literary and critical consciousness of his time" (Smallwood, *Philosophy of Enchantment*, xxv). Other personal experiences might have contributed such as the importance of fairy tales in the quotidian life of his family home; his father's ability as a composer and story teller; the ideas of the Victorian art critic John Ruskin who was a friend of the household (Collingwood's father had also been his secretary); the poet W.B. Yeats who used for his poems material gathered from the rich tradition of myths, folklore and legends of his native Ireland (Smallwood, *Philosophy of Enchantment*, xxv-xxvi). All these are no doubt good explanations as to why Collingwood was attracted to these stories.

6 Collingwood, *Religion and Philosophy*, xiii.

7 Ibid., xiii.

8 Collingwood, "Fascism and Nazism," 168.

9 Collingwood, *Philosophy of Enchantment*, 115.

10 Ibid.

11 Ibid., 116.

12 Ibid., 117.

13 For these issues see ibid., 120-125.

14 Ibid., 124.

15 Ibid., 119.

16 Ibid.

17 Ibid.

18 Ibid., 130.

19 Originally published in 1868. Ruskin, *Works*, 236. Collingwood's father was Ruskin's secretary and Collingwood had written an interesting early essay on Ruskin's philosophy (Collingwood, *Ruskin's Philosophy*, 1-43)
20 Collingwood, *Philosophy of Enchantment*, 130.
21 Ibid., 137.
22 Ibid., 139.
23 Ibid., 139-40.
24 Ibid., 145.
25 Ibid.
26 Ibid., 148.
27 Ibid., 149.
28 Ibid., 151. Collingwood had something to say about the problems of using aetiological myths in his first book in 1916, *Religion and Philosophy*, (mainly 5-7). There he examined anthropological claims about religion and the use of aetiological myths which asserted that the story which explains a religious ritual is not a "part of the real religious impulse." (5) Assuming that this story, the aetiological myth, develops into creed, a paradox arises that "that creed, with all its theological and philosophical developments, is not an integral part of any religion at all." (5)
29 Collingwood, *Philosophy of Enchantment*, 152-55.
30 Ibid., 156-77.
31 Ibid., 169.
32 Ibid., 171.
33 Ibid.
34 Ibid., 176.
35 Ibid., 180.
36 Ibid.
37 Ibid.
38 Ibid., 181.
39 Ibid., 193.
40 Ibid., 181.
41 Ibid., 182.
42 A good place to begin would be *The Idea of History* and *The Principles of History*.
43 For instance "the historian uses the fragment [of ancient custom and belief] by reconstructing in his mind the life and thought of the people who have left him this sample of their work" (Collingwood, *Philosophy of Enchantment*, 128) or "All historical knowledge involves the recreation in the historian's mind of the past experience which he is trying to study" (Ibid., 128-9) or "to man his fellow-man is never a mere external object ... but something to be sympathized with, to be studied by penetrating into his thoughts and re-enacting those thoughts for oneself" (Ibid., 153) or that dreams can not be "conserved and renewed in any re-enactment" (Ibid., 171)
44 Ibid., 184. The exact sentence, from his *Tractatus Theologico-Politicus*, is "I have striven not to laugh at human actions, not to weep at them, nor to hate them, but to understand them." (Ibid., 184, ft. 3)
45 Ibid., 184-5.
46 Ibid., 185.
47 Ibid., 193.

48 Ibid.
49 Ibid.
50 Ibid., 186. The exact sentence, from his *Fifteen Sermons Preached at the Rolls Chapel*, is "Things and actions are what they are, and the consequences of them will be what they will be. Why then should we desire to be deceived?" (Ibid., 186, ft. 5)
51 Ibid., 189-93.
52 Ibid., 189.
53 Ibid., 190.
54 Ibid., 192.
55 Ibid., 193.
56 Ibid.
57 Ibid., 131.
58 For the preliminary sections (description, classification) see mainly ibid., 235-48; for the interpretation ibid., 249-59.
59 Ibid., 250.
60 Ibid.
61 Ibid., 251.
62 Ibid., 251-2.
63 Ibid., 255.
64 For Collingwood's analysis see mainly ibid., 253-9.
65 Ibid., 118.
66 Collingwood, *Autobiography*, 86.
67 Collingwood, "Philosophy of History," 6.
68 Collingwood, *The New Leviathan*. (*The New Leviathan* is written in 45 short chapters, each comprises several short, numbered paragraphs. It is customary to reference paragraphs. My quote is from page 13)

References

Collingwood, Robin George. *Religion and Philosophy*. London: Macmillan and Co. Ltd., 1916.

Collingwood, Robin George. *Ruskin's Philosophy. An Address delivered at the Ruskin Centenary Conference*. Kendal: Titus Wilson and Son Publishers, 1922.

Collingwood, Robin George. "The Philosophy of History." *Historical Association Leaflet*, no. 79 (London 1930): 1–16.

Collingwood, Robin George. *An Autobiography*. Oxford: Oxford University Press, 1939.

Collingwood, Robin George. "Fascism and Nazism." *Philosophy* 15, no. 58 (April 1940): 168–176.

Collingwood, Robin George. *The New Leviathan or Man, Society, Civilization and Barbarism*. Oxford: Oxford Clarendon Press, 1942 (Revised Edition with an introduction and additional material edited by David Boucher, 1993).

Collingwood, Robin George. *The Idea of History*. Oxford: Oxford University Press, 1946 (Revised edition with Lectures 1926-1928, edited with an introduction by Jan van der Dussen, Oxford: Oxford University Press, 1994).

Collingwood, Robin George. *The Principles of History. And other writings in philosophy of history,* edited with an introduction by William Herbert Dray and W. Jan van der Dussen. Oxford: Oxford Clarendon Press, 1999.

Collingwood, Robin George. *The Philosophy of Enchantment. Studies in Folktale, Cultural Criticism, and Anthropology,* edited by David Boucher, Wendy James, and Philip Smallwood. Oxford: Oxford University Press, 2005.

Ruskin, John. *The Works of John Ruskin. Vol. 19: The Cestus of Aglaia and the queen of the air: with other papers and lectures on art and literature, 1860-1870,* edited by Edward Tyas Cook and Alexander Wedderburn. London: George Allen, 1905.

Part II

4 Romantic historiography and myths

We have seen that Collingwood had quite unambiguously claimed that the help of myths and fairy tales could be summoned in any historical reconstruction of the past. The right method was needed to do that and he offered some methodological directions. What this method indicated was not only the necessity of the technicalities in dealing with the subject matter but also a certain disposition towards it. This was a historical development of tremendous significance which had already occurred before Collingwood's time, it was the achievement of the Romantic movement. The technical problems had been addressed in a sophisticated way by people like Niebuhr and Savigny.[1] The new methods, however, had become possible and even necessary because of the realisation that history is important for understanding human conduct. This general disposition was now to go beyond generalisations and schematic histories if something more meaningful about human cultures were to be found. It was, therefore, not a mere accident that a major part of what may be called the "romantic revolution was the romantic revaluation of myths" and that while the Enlightenment had examined myth "in order to discredit it" Romanticism "assented to and celebrated myth."[2] The mythological revival was a corollary of Romanticism's appreciation of culture. Myth was seen as an intrinsic part of culture and not as a strange relic which had to be discarded since it could not be adequately explained in terms of a generic and abstract human rationality. In the following sections some themes of Romanticism will be explored in relation to its historiographical spirit and to some forgotten historical contributions, and to how that period stimulated some important developments in the study of myth. This is offered in a more general methodological tone, as general lines for a future study in mythology. For, despite these crucial developments the historical potential of mythology in the end remained largely unfulfilled. A major interest in myth during the Romantic period often came from literature and

DOI: 10.4324/9781315387703-6

philosophy and not historiography. As a result myth was used for poetic and symbolic purposes, or for creating grand visions which elevated myth to a position from where its historical roots were no longer visible.

* * *

For myths to move away from all those interpretative errors, it would require to understand how the conditions responsible for the previous obscurity came to be –at least temporarily– dispelled. This was an important step in the development of a historical way of understanding and in the creation of an alternative epistemological perspective. Giambattista Vico had played a very important part in initiating this operation. With regard to the study of myths and remote antiquity Vico argued that he had established "the only principles of mythology according to which the fables bore historical evidence as to the first Greek commonwealths, and by their aid ... all the fabulous history of the heroic commonwealths"[3] could be explained. Vico's power, however, to effect a serious change was quite marginal during his lifetime. His story is, therefore, routinely told through the discovery of his work by later currents of thought and the influence his ideas had on them. In particular it has been noted that Vico in his anti-rationalism and his belief that the conceptual and methodological structures of the natural sciences, already dominant during his lifetime, were unsuitable for the study of human affairs "anticipated the positions of Hamann and Herder and Burke, and the romantic movement."[4] Romanticism cordially received Vico's ideas because it had itself already made tangible and significant advancements towards a profounder understanding of history. These two lines, Vico and Romanticism, converge conceptually and also chronologically, to the extent that Romanticism introduced and diffused Vico to a wider circle of influences.

It has also been argued that the rediscovery of Vico's work, neglected for many years, "formed part of the Romantic revival of interest in the mythical and the non-logical."[5] Here the idea of non-logical should be understood as some form of resistance to "the cold and clinical perspectives associated with rationalism."[6] Resistance that led to the refinement of rationalism and thus to an expanded historical understanding. The mythical and the non-logical are aspects of Romanticism's wider perspective with regard to the past: myths as an intriguing feature of past societies which had been causing interpretative chaos for centuries, and the non-logical as an actual component of rationality itself. The strict opposition sometimes stipulated between logical and non-logical elements, to indicate the reasoned and the emotional self, has been a philosophical impasse. Romanticism tried to point out that seeing the self divided so neatly into distinct components was problematic. The recognition that human beings as such are only intermittently reliable and reasonable and the possibility that a certain element of malevolence may indeed exist within each individual, lay out a disturbing reality to encounter and accept unquestionably. A reality that is very complicated to explain, or try to explain away by abstract analytical categories and dualistic classifications. Perhaps occasional, undue emphasis on the emotional aspect may have given the impression that Romanticism was equally guilty of exploiting the same abstract categories and interpretations, just reversing them. While there is indeed some truth in this view, on the whole it may not be an accurate description of Romanticism. The Romantic historiography and political philosophy, for instance, are in the main free from such contradictions. Sometimes Romanticism is seen as comprising a "disparate sets of facts and tendencies"[7] and while it touched a number of fields (art, literature, religion, economics, science, morality, history, politics, philosophy) its influence did not establish unified principles and characteristics, let alone a specific course of action. In this sense Romanticism was "not a movement in the ordinary sense of a program adopted by a group."[8] Neat and overarching definitions of Romanticism may, thus, be difficult. Perhaps it would be preferable not so much to distinguish between different senses of Romanticism, as to speak of instances where the qualities of a common theme tend to be more or less present. And almost invariably the common theme of Romanticism is described as a new mood or consciousness which changed profoundly the existing balance of the European spirit. But consciousness of what exactly?

The meanings of Romanticism

Romanticism is sometimes used as a term of abuse, as something that is quite exalted, too volatile, emotional, immoderate, almost uncontrollable, that came to disrupt previous certainties and orthodoxies, and it was even ready to break ties with some aspects of reason and rationality in search of a more real or true self. It has been described as the "outburst against abstract reason and the search for order"[9] (against abstract reason but not reason as such) and in one of the most well known objections by Isaiah Berlin it was regarded as a crisis, a turning-point, a revolution, even at times a sinister phenomenon "in the history of Western political thought, and indeed more widely, in the history of human though and behaviour in Europe."[10] Berlin rather gravely, ominously and with a certain sentimentality maintained that,

the eighteenth century saw the destruction of the notion of truth
and validity in ethics and politics, not merely objective or absolute
truth, but subjective and relative truth also - truth and validity as
such - with vast and indeed incalculable results. The movement we
call romanticism transformed modern ethics and politics in a far
more serious way than has been realised.[11]

It is not always quite clear how to understand this total destruction or
whether it is even possible to support the notion that truth is not just
relative, subjective and questionable but entirely non existent. The idea
that even subjective truth can be destroyed and, in some sense, replaced by a notion which is neither truth nor falsehood, would, most
likely, render any relevant utterances almost incomprehensible. Also
very difficult to transmit to other people without causing the entire
structure of communication to collapse. Berlin's assessment is an ex-
aggeration but we may, however, keep from it the significance of
Romanticism as an event. It may or may not be "the greatest single
shift in the consciousness of the West that has occurred"[12] but it was
"a movement which was to change the consciousness of Europe"[13] The
emphasis on Romanticism predominantly as a state of consciousness
or as a "spiritual phenomenon"[14] is a recurring image, which occasionally intensifies Romanticism's mystical quality and erratic reputation. It is also a rather vague description and Barzun's version of
it as "a state of consciousness, exhibiting the divisions found in every
age"[15] does not really achieve any more clarity or precision. At the
same time there is nothing fundamentally wrong with defining
Romanticism as a form of consciousness. It is usually by such rather
imprecise terms and characterisations that we gradually achieve
more exactness and focus. We delineate historical periods by defining
their spirit, which is thought to be recognisable and distinct and thus
we separate one historical period from another. Thus the general
attitude and orientation of a period becomes somehow real: against
it the attribution of motives, specific ways of thinking and acting, etc.
can be justified. It is as if the spirit of an age, when it becomes explicit enough, dictates the conduct of the historical actors. The terms
spirit, consciousness, mood, disposition, temperament, a particular
turn of mind, something that even embodies particular feelings, all
these indicate something that often can not be described in more
concrete terms but at the same time may communicate enough information to make a certain point lucid. Still, such lucidity is more
common when describing other historical periods. Eras such as the
Renaissance and the Enlightenment have specific characteristics,

their own spirit, and are distinct and recognisable periods, and the term consciousness, if ever applied to them, is not used in the same way as when applied to Romanticism, it does not somehow carry the same intensity and confusion. The consciousness of Romanticism seems to be more evasive and unclear, its spiritual dimension expresses a strange and uneasy metaphysics. Also it would seem that any attempt to define the Romantic consciousness in terms of its content is problematic. Having quite distinct fields of enquiry expressing a common consciousness would require at least some unifying elements or characteristics towards which, however vaguely, this consciousness is directed or in terms of which it can be described. All those distinct fields, in other words, should have been able to exemplify this consciousness, permeated by a common message or motif. But since Romanticism meant so many different things to people who participated in that movement,[16] to locate something quite specific of which they were collectively conscious does not seem possible.

It may be the case that all the earlier discussions have unnecessarily complicated the issue. This mysterious quality may not be as mysterious, Romanticism is after all an established term and it conveys a certain meaning to everyone. One way, therefore, out of this confusion would be to acknowledge that with all concepts and categories a certain ambiguity will always be present. What is more, any historical period or movement which claims to be different and distinct is never fully free from past elements. It is a process, a transition which always inherits features from previous stages and bequeaths features to subsequent stages, often to be confused as features created by that particular stage. This may create internal contradictions especially when people of a certain period wish to point out their uniqueness at the expense of the similarities with a previous period. The spirit or consciousness of a certain period can be expressed in more solid terms, as the attempt to find the point where novelty and the differences outweigh the old and the similarities. It is never a precise affair since historical change is not precise either. But the moment we start thinking about what is one of the most defining features of the Romantic period, its expanded or heightened historical dimension seems quite convincing. Through the variety of Romanticism's themes and intentions everything assumes a strong historical quality. The quest for a "truer self", for instance, may easily become sentimental. But it remains sober as a historical pursuit by the extension of man's understanding to include emotional aspects and by going back to examine past societies and different mentalities and thus construct a comparative and broader picture of humanity. The "passionate protest against universality of any kind"[17] is again an affirmation of the historicity of things. At the same time this historicity did not need to adopt any categories of relativism, let alone to abolish criteria and discard notions of truth and validity as Berlin had feared. This is a common, and somehow justifiable, misapprehension but one that undermines and contradicts the historical spirit of Romanticism.

It is, of course, true that in Romanticism there is no real tension between different value systems as such because there is no attempt, at first, to compare any such systems. The historical spirit of Romanticism is an enquiry into the historical presuppositions of culture and not an enquiry into the realm of values, thus it begins by accepting that any cultural enquiry may stay within the bounds of facts. There is already an enormous amount of work to be done in trying to understand how different cultural systems operate, without any further attempt to look comparatively into the differences between various cultures and establish whether universal values exist or not. But there is nothing to imply that Romanticism denies that such values may exist and there is nothing to indicate that Romantic thinkers would have had a problem to choose between values. As a rule they had a preference for smaller, more coherent and "organic" societies as opposed to the advancing centralised, bureaucratic structures that were to dominate the post revolutionary world. This also implies a clear preference for an entire host of values which underscore these different society conceptions. The Romantics would have had no hesitation to proclaim the values of the smaller societies as universally valid.

In addition, although it involves primarily understanding and not comparison or the attempt to define the absolute, the Romantic historical spirit aspired to historical knowledge. This knowledge is not just about explaining how different cultures operate but also about establishing how successful they have been in doing so. All societies exhibit traits of success or failure in their cultural practices and any historical knowledge would be truncated and incomplete without this element. In the historical spirit of Romanticism there are implicit (if not quite explicit) criteria, norms and ways to ascertain and judge the success or failure of those cultural practices, including their more theoretical and value related aspects. Historical understanding is never completely factual. Soon enough such questions as "What does this activity mean? What are those people trying to achieve?" will be followed by an attempt to answer another set of questions "Has this activity been successful? Have those people achieved what they were trying to achieve?" The activity may be successful or unsuccessful, or only partially successful, in terms of producing any practical results, or of advancing a better theoretical understanding and explanation of reality. But for an external observer the success or failure would be judged according to criteria that the observer most certainly considers universally valid. Romanticism by accepting cultural pluralism does not necessarily deny universality. To do so would subvert the main purpose of Romanticism's historical spirit: the attainment of historical knowledge. For Romanticism historical knowledge is not the source of useful and expedient lessons to be enjoyed by the present, but human self knowledge. Learning about past societies and ancient modes of thinking offers various approximations of the capabilities of the human spirit. Ideally these approximations would yield a deeper, more fundamental image of what it is to be human. But to do so the approximations should be judged as to their efficacy to produce such a deeper image. This judgement requires, therefore, criteria that have some claim to universality. This is certainly a formidably difficult process and not a very rewarding task. The main difficulty is that we are constantly faced with approximations and potentialities and the idea of a more perfect and true picture of ourselves is forever escaping our reach. But it is out of these approximate selves that we hope to be able at some point to construct something deeper. We ceaselessly strive and the challenge remains open.

The historical mindedness of Romanticism

According to R.G. Collingwood the advancement of historical thought during the Romantic period was made possible because of two elements.[18] First, a wider and more sympathetic investigation as to include also various past ages which had been previously neglected, scorned and remained obscure by the historical thought of the Enlightenment which treated (or for that matter ignored) vast areas of history as barbaric and undeserving of serious attention; the second element was that the concept of the immutability of human nature had to be revised as to show that it was not static, uniform, and unchanging. Past historical periods could now be understood quite differently: as possessing permanent value of their own and exhibiting a unique achievement, and also as valid stages in the development of human civilisation. The intense sympathy for the Middle Ages found in Romantic writers, such as Sir Walter Scott, when contrasted with the lack of sympathy for the same period by Enlightenment writers, such as David Hume, shows "how this tendency of the Romanticism had enriched its historical outlook."[19] Collingwood further argues that the interest, admiration and sympathy that the Romantics tended to have for the past may be seen as resembling the appreciation of the humanists for Greco-Roman antiquity. But this resemblance is rather extrinsic. The admiration of the Romantics is genuine and profound, since in various past achievements they recognised and valued "the spirit of their own past"[20] as opposed to the humanists who would only search for models for imitation, but deep down they "despised the past as such."[21]

The Romantic historical consciousness with its different appreciation of the past was, therefore, a necessary corrective to an established, and at times severely distorted, view of human circumstances and the development of human societies. Romanticism "founded modern historiography, interpreting it no longer as mockery and derision of past ages, but as understanding of these as parts of the present and of the future."[22] The previously held view of history, dominant from the Renaissance onward, had two additional flaws which made the past and any historical knowledge defective. The first was the past's expected efficacy as a teacher of historical and moral lessons: when such lessons were to be had the past was a source of limited wisdom, otherwise it could be safely dismissed. The second flaw was the confusion as a clear consequence of the ongoing competition between the historical and the scientific spirits.

It has been argued that history "in the eighteenth century both went into decline and flourished as never before."[23] As far as it did exhibit a certain interest in the past, the Enlightenment and the eighteenth century in general, was not an antihistorical period and "in the later eighteenth century no subject was more read or written about than history."[24] However it held a not very dissimilar view of history to that of the Humanists and on the whole it treated the past with suspicion. The Enlightened philosophers believed that history should be studied instrumentally, either to show how bad the past has been or in order to "disengage general facts"[25] and thus provide useful lessons for the present. Such conception does not support a proper historical interest in the past. It wishes to dissect the past as to separate useful from non useful things, upsetting thus its integrity and its coherence. The past dissected in this artificial manner, and cut off from a more meaningful connection with the present and indeed with the future too, can not speak with its authentic voice but will utter whatever the transient fancies of the present wish to hear. If the present uses the past in such a way it will not really benefit from it. The alleged lessons will not (and can not) be genuine for it is assumed that what worked under certain circumstances will always work. This again requires a weird understanding of human nature, not so much immutable as selectively desirable: some aspects of it are coveted while some others better to be avoided. There is a curious lack of humility here, to believe that we deserve to be given everything that is good in our nature but to try to avoid its dark forces. If we engage seriously with the past we may be able to receive its gift, which is historical understanding and in a more broad sense human self knowledge. If we do actually receive those things we will know all too well that we are made in a way more likely to resist than to be amenable to past, or any other, wisdom.

Another way of finding the past useful was to detect those elements which had contributed to an alleged progress and had paved the way to the current state of things. The assumption is that progress favours aspects of the present, and it is in order to celebrate them and trace the course that led to them that some historical elements will be selected and others discarded, according to how well they support or not this notional progress. This procedure is of course crude and arbitrary, because there is no genuine way to remove pieces from the past and leave others in place without disturbing the intricate links that connect the various stages of the historical process. Romanticism halted those impersonal forces and its historians were now "eager to describe not the mechanics of progress, which so easily led to revolution, but the robust vitalising spirit which fortified and preserved the legitimate organs, institutions, and traditions of the past."[26] In doing so it also resurrected the individuals who had been hitherto cast aside or subsumed under the tide of the doctrine of progress. Those simple men of the past had "entered their story only indirectly, as the agents or victims of 'progress': they seldom appeared directly, in their own right, in their own social context, as the legitimate owners of their own autonomous centuries."[27] The romantic writers changed that, the legitimacy of the individual became another Romantic achievement, so often announced in previous historical periods but only partially or imperfectly realised.

It might seem hard to reconcile the aforementioned two views of history and the past held by the Enlightenment. On the one hand as something generally bad, untrustworthy, that elicits suspicion, and on the other hand as having utility because it can provide some general facts to guide present and future actions. This is clearly an early positivistic attitude, seeing individual facts as instances of general rules. And this brings us to the clash between the scientific and the historical attitudes mentioned earlier, and the resulting confusion that came out of it. The Enlightenment was the recipient of the seventeenth century's advancements in science and it was this new scientific spirit with which every field of knowledge, produced during the Enlightenment, was infused. It was not history that guided knowledge and understanding but science. And whenever history appeared during that period it was not real history but something that had to conform to the scientific ideal. Thus it was to the influence of the Enlightenment that "we can readily trace the origins of a school ... that wished to see history as social science."[28] History as social science had many logical inconsistencies and Romanticism inaugurated a period of historical ascendancy to counterbalance the theoretical, epistemological and even ethical predominance of science and to correct some of these inconsistencies. It had to "thrust back into their natural limits the natural and mathematical sciences and their correlative mental form, showing that, outside of their own field, they were impotent to resolve the antinomies with which the mind came into conflict."[29] One such antinomy would be that any approach that sees history as a form of science usually favours a value free enquiry. In that sense history becomes a descriptive science and the lessons of the past, the general facts about the human condition, would be of little use as guiding principles, even when the existence of a constant human nature is postulated. A value free, general fact about human beings is possible but it would take the form of a biological or physiological fact. To establish anything useful in terms of human behaviour and human conduct it would have to place one in the position of an acting or responding agent, who has to consider a wealth of relevant information of the specific situation in order to act or respond to it. Any general fact about human conduct, taken not from history but from the idea of history as science, reduces the actions and responses of an agent into formulaic and mechanistic happenings. This may be adequate enough for the idea of a value free creature that things simply occur to it, but it does not describe any actual human being. In sharp contrast Romanticism tried "to produce a history that was creative and alive and the reverse of value-free."[30] A history that not only describes and tries to understand facts, actions and events but also judges and appraises a vast and complicated range of motives, intentions and the like. This is not a value free enquiry and certainly not one where criteria of truth and validity have been abolished.

The idea of human nature seems to underlie some of the earlier points discussed. This is a topic which can very quickly move to many different directions assisted by an enormous number of related topics and by a deep ancestry. But a modest point could be made with regard to the historical suppositions of Romanticism. It is a common enough thought that Romanticism denied the existence of human nature as such, and in seeing human beings as historical it accepts that they are determined or even totally constructed by history and culture, by things that we learn and not by something that we are. It is easy to see how this view has been propagated in this dualistic form. The assumption behind it is that there are essentially two ways to see human beings and that they oppose each other. One has it that they are part of nature and as such they participate in the realm of natural things, the specific forms of which "constitute a changeless repertory of fixed types."[31] These fixed types can be found everywhere and in every period and exhibit essentially the same basic characteristics, deviations are possible but still within a recognisable and predictable range. The other way is that history and culture have a special power to mould people and thus different cultural environments and historical periods have been able to create different human beings. People now are malleable, ever changing and unpredictable. Thus a constant, reliable, measurable, human nature does not exist, history and culture are our only hopes to navigate through this impossible maze. Occasionally a compromise seems desirable: there is indeed a variety of distinct forms of human activity, but there is also something to unite them. The seemingly dissimilar and unrelated, and often genuinely original, utterances are nonetheless manifestations of the same human urges. This well known identity-in-difference motif is very real as in every case we contrast aspects of one and the same thing: the human being. When we speak of human beings as fundamentally the same (sharing a common human nature) in the face of noticeable differences, either geographical or historical, we affirm this reality. Conversely, when we say that those differences between human beings should confirm that they do not have a common nature, we are instantly drawn back to doubt by denying that what is the same (a human being) is not indeed the same. There is of course a real problem affirming the human nature unequivocally, as there are striking examples of differences that can not be easily attributed to the same source which produces cultural variants. There are cultural achievements so astounding that we can not easily understand their inception. Human nature and culture, as sub categories of the problems of understanding in general, remain largely enigmatic. But there is always the impulse to persevere. Butterfield had captured something of the strains and peculiarities of historical understanding when he stated that,

> The primary assumption of all attempts to understand the men of the past must be the belief that we can in some degree enter into minds that are unlike our own. If this belief were unfounded it would seem that men must be for ever locked away from one

another, and all generations must be regarded as a world and a law unto themselves.[32]

What was, therefore the view of Romanticism about human nature? We might say that Romanticism stressed the importance of culture and the emphasis was turned away from human nature as such. Different societies exhibit their potentialities in various ways but they are still part of a continuum, a historical process where every culture leaves a certain impression. In that sense Romanticism regards cultures and civilisations as universal things, succession of stages in mankind's quest for clarity, each contributing something. Without this common thread any relation between those phases would be lost. The historical process would become inchoate, unable to process and translate human action into anything more substantive than a modicum within the mass of undifferentiated experience.

* * *

Romanticism's major accomplishment was that, to a certain extent, it managed to halt the advancement of the mechanistic conception of man. The Romantic period brought to the fore certain wider pre-suppositions of this conception. One interpretation would be to say that the difficulty with the mechanistic human being was not that it possesses a human nature but that it possesses a mechanistic human nature. Nature had replaced God and now human nature is part of Nature. The mechanistic world view is a scheme where Nature and everything in it can not be judged normatively: Nature became infallible. Before God was infallible but human beings were not. Now as parts of the mechanistic view of Nature are, in a sense, infallible. The name for this human infallibility is reason. The emphasis on reason was the emphasis on the innate infallibility of man. Seeing human beings as infallible intensifies the awe which occurs when they do inevitably fail. As it is hard to explain things in terms of a failure of reason, the opposite happens instead: the explanation is that people merely failed to apply reason. Why this malfunction occurs, why people act unreasonably, is very difficult to explain and it is the Achilles heal of any conception which sees human beings as infallible.

The truth is that people do not actually act reasonably or unreasonably, logically or illogically, rationally or irrationally. They act more concretely than that: they act honourably or dishonourably, cowardly or heroically and so forth. We may wish to say that to act honourably or heroically is the reasonable thing to do. But this is again unsatisfactory. Because to define something as reasonable or unreasonable we need criteria, and reason can not establish such criteria because it pretends to be non-normative: the assumed "faculty" of reason is nothing more that the justification of man's infallibility as a part of a mechanistic and infallible Nature. We can retain, if we wish, the term reason but only as an ornamental category. But to answer why an honourable action has been reasonable we would need to bring forward criteria as to what acting in an honourable manner actually means. This may not be easy either, but it is the only way to define and understand concrete human action.

Replacing God with a mechanistic Nature produced a confused picture. Under any transcendent view human beings could be good but they could also offend. They had fallen and their subsequent story became one of toil and constant plea for redemption. The mechanistic conception of man created the illusion that human beings were infallible. This appears to be quite an extraordinary assertion but it is a consequence of the mechanistic view of the world, where everything will be fine as long as we realise that we are reasonable and rational beings and exercise our reason. Understanding any transgressions of reason became, in most cases, incomprehensible. A naïve arrogance about the rationality of the present and a belief in progress and the continuation of reason, was coupled with a profound contempt for the past which had made no use of the gift of reason. Present man and past man became competing shadows in a vast theatre of impossibilities.

Romanticism's heightened sense of historical consciousness was a sober and much needed expansion of aspects which had become obsolete under the overly rational view of the Enlightenment's thinkers. It pointed out that any previous historical spirit was only superficially resembling historical as it had become too dependent on scientific ways of thinking, slowly transforming history into a form of science. Romanticism changed the excessively mechanistic conception of man and enlarged the field of potential sources for the study of history, culture and the past. And it did this not because there was necessarily a corresponding factual enlargement, new historical evidence previously unavailable. The Enlightenment had seen significant new historical information becoming available but its historical understanding was such that it treated the new as additional instances of the already known. The changes of Romanticism were important but they were not radical as frequently the main requirement for historical understanding is something more simple and subtle. Each generation may engage afresh with almost the same historical problems mainly by accepting that the "growth of historical knowledge ... comes about not by adding new facts to those already known, but by transforming the old ideas in the light of the new."[33] The new historical awareness of Romanticism made possible to reinterpret and appreciate many departments of knowledge previously condemned to oblivion as illogical and conceptual errors. No manifestation of human culture could be seen as otiose, including myths. After a significant period of relative neglect and misinterpretations, a resurgent interest could revisit the former historical claims of myths and retrieve their lost connection with a narrative which somehow aspired to truth. Voltaire had believed that "myths are 'the ravings of savages and the inventions of knaves,' or at best harmless fancies conjured up by poets to charm their readers."[34] Quite contrary to that Romanticism was prepared to confront myths, from the outset, as an indication of a genuine, deliberate, and purposeful activity. Moreover as an activity that exemplifies a degree of intelligibility. To be able to differentiate between an attempt (even an unsuccessful one, and perhaps sometimes especially an unsuccessful one since a failed attempt may be easily confused with an error) at a specific activity and an error would depend on knowing what the question was to which that attempt was meant to provide an answer. Finding the right question would mean to try to ask, ideally, the same question as the one the people who were performing the past activity had asked. In simple terms we would need to understand what they were doing and what it meant for them. Asking the correct questions and getting the nature of the activity right is not easy and silent assumptions often lead to misunderstandings. This is a common methodological and conceptual confusion. But something similar also happens when a defective attitude towards the past in general is being employed. We have seen that one of the most common such distortions of the past was to see it as a blueprint or inspiration for the present. To consider, that is, only some of its aspects as relevant and alive, the rest as dead and unimportant. Another way to distort the past would be to see it merely in an antiquarian way. Antiquarian not in the sense understood by those semi-amateurs scholars and enthusiasts, who were seriously engaged with the past *as* past, deeply fond of it, always trying to understand its secrets and patiently listening to its weary voices. Antiquarian in the sense of a distant and exotic spectacle with an impressive array of curious and quite preposterous relics. It is a common place that a past thus understood is a dead past. The past will only make sense when taken as the implied reality – difficult, challenging and dear – of the people who lived in it. The past as it was for them, their present, pertinent and valuable. This is a past which is alive not dead. It is the life of something that is no longer with us. But as a historical past, it is not dead. In a very real sense the only experience we have is that of creation and life. Death is a mystery not a part of experience and thus incomprehensible. We can not study something as if it were dead and expect to make sense of it. Previous periods may be seen as approximations towards historical understanding, but not particularly successful. It is not an accusation to say that those historical periods had an imperfect historical understanding or that they fell under the spell of scientific and not historical thinking. As historical periods they were what they were and tried to make sense of themselves and reality as best as they could. But the fact remains that they misunderstood the past and almost all of its facets, especially myths, and saw history not as a process of which they were also a part, but as the onward movement that had culminated in their exalted present. It is with the advent of Romanticism and its corollaries that a spectrum of notions came together and inaugurated a more genuine historical understanding. In what follows three of them will be discussed: the concept of historical change, the concept of historical cosmopolitanism, and the concept of unity of the mind and the peculiar sense of freedom attached to it. These features by no means exhaust the portrait of the historical perspective but they do, however, capture something of Romanticism's understanding of what it means to see things historically. The reinvigoration of the study of myths is a part of this story.

Historical change

An important aspect of the historical dimension of Romanticism is how it perceived the notion of change. It may be said that there can not be a society, which understands itself in historical terms, that at the same time does not conceive change in such terms as well. And it seems to be a historical premise that change is by definition inevitable and unavoidable: the future *will* be different from the present and the past. How different societies respond to such a conception of change is complicated. It is usually assumed that more traditional societies are averse to change. That, although inevitable, change should be made to be slow, resisted as much as possible, be under judicious control or dispensed only when absolutely necessary. In contrast it is thought that more progressive societies, where strong tradition is not ne-cessarily a decisive factor of organisation, frequently operate under the more confident assumption that the inevitability of change is also reason to welcome it and that to a great extent change is malleable and may be produced at will or at least we may influence its direction. Now this description may be true up to a certain point, namely that more traditional societies see the inevitability of change negatively, while less traditional, and more progressive, societies understand change, broadly speaking, in a more positive way. But, perhaps surprisingly, it is not a society's traditional or progressive character which dictates a society's attitude towards change. It is the exact opposite, that is, it is a society's attitude towards change which determines whether that society will be more traditional or more progressive.

There are societies where the awareness of the inevitability of historical change is seen as an invitation to participate in it full-heartedly. It is a process that may be difficult but it is also a promise of or an opportunity for something better, a hope that the future will be not just inevitable but better. Change becomes synonymous to progress. It is no wonder that we call these societies progressive, they see the historical change and the historical formation of societies with a speculative twist, history as having a plan and a direction both of which are positive. This attitude has little to do with optimism as such, because the assertion that things will be better is being made not just with confidence but with certitude.

In contrast a different awareness of historical change occurs more strongly in those societies where, for various reasons (perhaps size, conception of vulnerability, historical trajectory, cultural norms, values etc.), the historicity of our social set ups is understood as a relentless, chaotic unfolding which depends upon a complicated and unpredictable combination of factors. These societies realise how precarious their social and their political arrangements at any given moment are. Thus they do not welcome change and try to resist it, although they acknowledge how futile it would be to try to escape it. We tend to call such societies traditional. They are not averse to change because they are traditional, they become traditional because of an uncomfortable awareness of what historical change might have in store for them.

To the extent that historical change is inevitable but its direction unknown, both these responses are legitimate. What is more, discussing change in terms of societies does not mean that individuals are of secondary importance or that societies are uniform in their attitude towards change. In fact both the traditional and the progressive attitudes coexist within the same society and one or the other becomes more dominant depending on prevailing orthodoxies and individual choices. The role of people as historical agents is very important in this respect. The inevitability of historical change seems to suggest that no matter what we do and think change is a force which can withstand our orchestrated efforts to artificially influence the course of things. Therefore change as a historical category is effectively placed beyond one's real control or one's desire to either stall or hasten it. But this is exactly what both traditional and progressive societies habitually do: they try to meddle with change, either resist it or assist it.

In societies we call traditional, which recognise the force of historical change as something not altogether desirable, the attempt to meddle with change takes the form of resistance through tradition and the promotion of incremental, personal change. These societies seem to believe that desirable, and thus real, change is the one connected with individual sovereignty and effected through the actions of the individual. Since historical change will certainly occur and the individual desire for life and action will also produce further change, tradition and individual change are mechanisms to limit the potential impact of the overall change. In such societies tradition expresses the relation between change and the desire for stability and changelessness and it assists the unavoidable transition from one to the other. It is difficult to understand tradition as something different than protection against the unpredictable consequences of change. For such societies change is a historical process safeguarded by tradition.

But what is tradition? Tradition is a link between the present and the past, a continuity which helps people to form a clearer idea of the historical origins and nature of their society. Tradition is created, comes to be, through a convoluted and in many respects incomprehensible process and in a sense it fights back against the arbitrariness of this process by resisting change as much as possible. Thus a strange equilibrium is maintained between the uncertainty of having become something, having reached a certain stage, and the desire to stay as it is and change no more. It is an ungrateful process and the equilibrium is fragile, to say the least. But it is one of the ways to explain tradition as being aware of historical change (for the complexity of tradition is otherwise difficult to account for) and at the same time a proponent of immutability. Tradition bears the burden of this complexity, demonstrating by its very existence what the actual actions of past and present societies amount to: an intricate weave of innumerable elements that assumed a unique and unrepeatable appearance for each society, out of the infinity of possible forms and combinations. Hence it is somehow wrong to associate tradition with obstinate preservation of things that they should have long gone. Tradition's job was to hold on to everything, it has recorded the development of history for particular societies. It would be up to us to select, to reform, to discard. It is a difficult task and one which we often feel guilty to perform out of respect for tradition, which means we are guilty to upset the delicate balance of the totality of the things that compose our experiences and our existence, of which totality we understand very little. In the face of the inevitability of historical change which falls out of our control, tradition shows that any other further change we wish to effect should not be on a large scale, thus compounding the unpredictable consequences of the future. The only alternative is limited, personal change as it will most likely upset any future equilibrium as little as possible.

The opposite seems to be the case in those societies we call progressive, that regard the inevitability of historical change as an opportunity to enact progress. As the outcome of any historical change is indeed unknown such societies choose to assist this process by concerted and collective efforts. These efforts usually involve ambitious schemes for societal transformation, large scale changes, planning and clearly delineated outcomes. Such an attitude towards change would not, however, really know where to begin, any starting point would be equally arbitrary and the outcomes uncertain. Combining large scale change with the inevitability of historical change will create a force difficult to predict, which has often resulted in serious imbalances and grievances. Although progressive societies may claim to understand that historical change is a part of any historical process, the employment of orchestrated changes and the belief in progress are signs that a society is convinced it may operate outside of the historicity of societal development. Change then becomes a matter of willing and planning, trying to force forward a process which is only partially understood and only partially under our control.

Contrary to what it is commonly assumed, traditional societies tend to understand and handle change better than progressive societies. Handling change is not only about instigating it but also about curtailing it. The attempt to remain as unaltered as possible requires effort and could be as dynamic and arduous as any attempt to change dramatically. In fact often is more so. Because maintaining the existing equilibrium means dealing with a concrete and real situation and not with something (substantial change) that is only desired and as yet not real but hypothetical. The notion that traditional societies, compared with progressive ones, risk very little when it comes to change is also erroneous. They actually risk more. They risk the loss of their settled ways that they hold dear and to which they are attached. They risk all they invested when they chose to understand their unique situation with its complexities, instead of dismantling it and replacing it with something else. It is more about being grateful for the present and respectful towards the past. The progressive societies, on the other hand, with their quest for drastic change and progress, and their predilection for the absolute, are more concerned with the future. Not particularly appreciative of the present and only very rarely pre-occupied with the past, they feel they do not have much to lose. Thus they do not risk much either and the potential consequences of a failure will be absorbed by the ongoing confidence that the next experiment in utopian bliss may be successful.

These given two conceptions or tendencies correspond with how Romanticism and the Enlightenment defined their attitudes towards change. The Enlightenment's was a belief in progress through changes on a large scale, done collectively, a feature of progressive societies. Romanticism understood the traditional societies and their strong historical sense and would favour personal change as the only way to lessen the unpredictability of the future. If it is understood that any historical process involves historical change which is inevitable and largely out of our influence, then the tension between historical change and forced, deliberate change becomes clear. Any theorising which purports to be historical and at the same time regards deliberate, collective actions as the main driving force for change, or describes change in terms of desirability of outcomes and attempts at progress, any such theorising operates under confused historical concepts. The collectivist impulse to drive things forward at will disregards the fact that all historical agents who wish to create or are involved in the conditions which may effect change, do so under certain restrictions, which make any planning precarious and any coveted outcome doubtful. This is not about pessimism or historical determinism. It is simply about human limitation and the tremendous complexity of the historical process.

Historical change as the negation of the concept of progress releases the real importance of the individual sovereignty. The individual, free from any obligations to a fictitious future moulded by progress, can be seen acting in ways compatible with the practical and theoretical considerations of life and not as contributions to the imaginary march towards progress. The negation of the concept of progress also creates a rightful place for all the stages of civilisation within humanity's historical development. Myths, in particular, may be understood as a component of this process, a valuable expression of a certain era and of a certain mode of thinking. Romanticism by approaching myths historically managed to offset, at least for some time, years of established opinions which regarded myths as illogical aberrations, outlandish stories, lies, misrepresentations of nature and reality and so forth. Romanticism has often been charged with a return to the irrational and the non-logical. If that implies that it tried to resurrect and revere myths precisely because they were a relic of irrational thinking, then this is clearly wrong. Romanticism's historical consciousness is nothing else but the belief that the past is intelligible because its activities were purposeful. That is not the same as to say that those activities were always successful, that they achieved what they set out to achieve. But it means that they were not at variance with all the conditions and qualities that would enable them to become understood. If this were the case the very idea of historical knowledge would be compromised and many activities of the past lost to us.

Historical cosmopolitanism

Another implication of Romanticism's heightened historical consciousness is that it offers real scope for embracing both the local and the ecumenical with almost equal confidence. It is upon realising the real value of other cultures and mentalities that Romanticism becomes cosmopolitan. This might be called historical cosmopolitanism, issuing, that is, from historical understanding of other societies, past or present. It has none of the leanings of the Enlightenment and similar views, which were often based on principles of abstract reasoning, trying to bring humanity under a common expectation by espousing the logic of uniformity over variation, local idiosyncrasies and individual historical developments.

The Enlightenment is often regarded as universal in its aspirations. At best it was an assumption that a set of values could be extended to those who had either already embraced of were willing to embrace the Enlightened principles. It was a highly eclectic and selective doctrine which excluded much, reluctant as it were to engage genuinely with various past cultures that were deemed to fall short of the Enlightened rationalism, quickly marked as superstitious and irrational. There is, of course, nothing unusual in the Enlightenment's request for compliance, and for abiding by the rules. All cultures are potentially inclusive systems, but they are also defined by what they wish to exclude. The term "community" (often used with regard to culture and often is made to mean something that should be indefinitely extended to include as much as possible) clearly denotes participation based on common values and characteristics. The Enlightenment was no different in this respect. But there are two observations to be made.

The first is that the Enlightenment's participation is often predicated on the idea of historical progress. In so far as progress favours always the present as the most current and successful version of this process, it is an achievement that comes with all the trappings of a narrow vision. Large areas of past human activities are excluded solely because they occurred in the past and not in the present. This makes any idea of historical cosmopolitanism impossible or very difficult. The idea, that is, to feel at home in the past and enjoy aspects of it. The second is that any idea of universality that the Enlightenment may put forward is severely restricted. Even within the western cultural sphere its appeal was not widespread because its anti religious and secular context, despite the secular advances in the post medieval period, was hardly in tune with the cultural heritage of Europe. The religious sentiment remained strong among a substantial number of European people. There is something to be said about a movement with universal aspirations that at the same time was intent on convincing people that their time honoured religious presuppositions were theoretically invalid and erroneous. Presuppositions which historically, if not also conceptually, had created one of the most stable set of values known, and enjoyed almost universal assent. In fact, a more obvious example of universalism was present in the Middle Ages, when societies seemed to organise themselves in terms of their shared religious faith and their commitment to the divine. This did not merely clarify for them their understanding of their place in the cosmos, alleviating the mysteries of existence, but offered practical guidance and values for their quotidian tasks. This foundation seems to have been stronger than anything the Enlightenment managed to achieve.

The universalism, therefore, of the Enlightenment was in many respects unreal as it had abolished values that for many people were more truly universal. Also it was not cosmopolitan either since cosmopolitanism recognises and wishes to retain the variety of different cultural expressions, including those of the past. The Enlightenment's ambition was to bring everything under the aegis of one rationality, it hoped to increase the boundaries of the familiar. Instead of feeling comfortable and at home in different environments, it would try to bring those environments to resemble home as closely as possible. In reality the Enlightenment was too uniform to be cosmopolitan, too narrow to be universal, but its confidence in its values and its desire to transmit them made it internationalist.

Any true historical cosmopolitanism can not be said to be a viable position on its own, one can not be a cosmopolitan if no differences and no distinctions exist. Cosmopolitanism can only be meaningful if it can be tested against a person's more localised loyalties and attachments. It requires tangible understanding of one's own standing and allegiances before one is willing to interact in earnest with different environments, to "appreciate human life in all its peaceful forms, and ... [to be] emotionally in touch with the customs, languages and cultures of many different people."[35] Forming a clear and confident idea about one's place and feeling comfortable within different environments is what cosmopolitanism requires and it is a demanding requirement. For it means that we must maintain not only these two identities but also the distinction between them if we are to understand them through their contrast, and also to be reasonably certain that they will not clash. True cosmopolitanism, therefore, is quite difficult to achieve and rather rare. Most encounters with alien ideas and habits can not disguise for long the fact that often the interplay between different cultural understandings is rather superficial and problematic, that it will remain rooted in hesitation, misunderstanding, lack of sympathy or empathy for the new, and sometimes strange, spectacles. These are all natural enough responses as the element of local attachment prevails and can not easily be abandoned in favour of something that we do not feel quite ours. Such responses are also necessary as mechanisms which create points of reference that navigate the individual self. If the attachment is repressed the sense of reality becomes warped and the individuals disorientated, feeling at home nowhere. If pushed too far any attachment becomes suffocating, unable to provide alternatives to a self that wants not only to be attached but occasionally to wander too.

This conflict reveals the deep tension between these two different aspects of the self. It also makes visible certain limits as to how far we can take our understanding of different cultural arrangements. There are certain barriers that simply can not be dissolved. It is a recurring theme that cultures define persons in ways that are impossible to break down and understand completely. Such persons become equipped with certain features and through them are connected with their cultural realities in a manner which can not be altered without the individual experiencing a significant amount of confusion and disarray. Subsequently, a person who comes to understand a different culture quite well, will also understand the impossibility of becoming a coequal member of that culture, of assuming a complete identity with it.

Romanticism came to accentuate this difficulty even further by stressing the importance of culture as a special way in which people could arrange and understand themselves. It made Europeans "take notice of the fact that each people spoke a specific language or dialect, enjoyed particular culinary tastes, customs, manners, artistic inheritance, and much else. A culture was a kind of spiritual rather than political body ... which expressed itself in poetry and song and was a unique modification of human possibility."[36] Cultural awareness is also associated with national awareness, with the expression of self determination of individual cultures. It may be argued, therefore, that Romanticism instead of bringing people closer it drove them hopelessly apart: cultural idiosyncrasies and distinct national identities could become factors that support isolationist tendencies. In one sense this is indeed conceivable if national awareness is understood in the dubious and much less profitable sense of nationalism, which refers to "the passionate solidarity of established states in their quarrels with others of their kind."[37] But there is precious little to suggest that Romanticism could have promoted such an idea. In fact Romantic nationalism is a precondition of Romantic cosmopolitanism. It is only when one's own origins are clear and secure that a meaningful contact with other cultural environments is possible. The realisation that one belongs to a distinct and unique culture gives also rise to the realisation that other cultures also exist and that make exactly the same claim. Then the question is how one culture may relate to another. Romanticism, because of its historical awareness, has a simple enough answer. Individual cultures should be understood as unique stages in the historical development and as such of equal interest to the study of human civilisation. Anyone interested in this broad civilisation would be appreciating life's variety and feeling at home in different cultural environments. The Romantic cosmopolitans may be "patriots of one country, but nationalists of many."[38]

The problem, however, remains. While Romanticism promotes historical cosmopolitanism and encourages people to delve into different cultures and try to understand them, a culture's idiosyncrasies seem almost impervious to total decipherment. Is, therefore, intercultural understanding ever possible? Romanticism's effort to restore the legitimacy of the emotional human nature, as something that it is not necessarily against the premises and requirements of rationality but complements it, provides a reasonable answer as to how different cultures could be approached. A culture is a type of "spiritual body" and as such its has elements that pertain to deeper needs which it may be said that all human beings have in common. Being in touch with a different culture means primarily to be emotionally in touch with it, to be reminded of the real nature of our commonalities with other people: human nature is first and foremost about emotional identity. It is also possible to approach a different culture in more intellectual, so to speak, terms but this will only reveal to us external features of the new customs and habits that we have come across. This understanding will be limited and fragmented as the different culture will remain a spectacle to us. Approaching a culture emotionally, on the other hand, we recognise it as something we can find within us too, as adjustments and potentialities of a common emotional source. Thus, while their particular details may be forever evading us, we will be able to appreciate different cultures and resume in good faith the quest for understanding them more, comfortable in the knowledge that what appears remote and strange is oddly familiar too. True historical cosmopolitanism, therefore, is not the attitude of complete and unquestionable understanding of different people and their cultures, but the realisation of the emotional affinity of humanity.

In summary. The historical cosmopolitanism of Romanticism accepted cultural variety and divergence as a fact and tried to show that it is possible to feel at ease within such cultural complexity. Instead of diminishing or bridging distinctions, it claimed that one should maintain cultural attachments arising out of specific historical contingencies, and explore other cultures with interest. The remotest a certain environment is from our familiar values the more challenging, vigorous and genuine historical cosmopolitanism may become. Because of the nature of culture some elements of one culture may always remain inaccessible to bearers of another, and perhaps similar (even historically related) cultural enclaves may be able to understand each other better. But common ground exists between cultures due to the emotional kinship between people. Cultures as predominantly spiritual bodies express and confirm deeper needs of people, needs that are primarily emotional in nature. With regard to myths the historical cosmopolitanism of Romanticism provides a more fruitful approach than the purely rationalistic ones which misunderstood and derided the mythical universe. Myth is cryptic and peculiar as a product of specific cultures, but also a pre-eminent example of the spiritual character which all cultures share. Any attempt to understand myths would require to be emotionally in touch with them, that is, to recognise in them an element we also possess, but an element somehow modified and adapted to the needs of the specific cultures that created and used myths. In some respect this element, in all its various manifestations, is how we relate to the transcendent.

Unity of the mind and freedom

Another point issuing from Romanticism's historical consciousness is what me may call the unity of the mind. The conception, that is, of individual cultures as self sufficient wholes, where every part, every activity, every manifestation of the spiritual life has its own place within the whole, and where each activity influences all other activities and in turn is influenced by all. The unity of a culture is not, however, always evident. Although cultures do have a certain consistency which makes them externally distinct and internally coherent, it was Romanticism that stressed further the autonomy and cohesion of cultures. This cohesion explains the various elements as parts of the whole. In a sense it could be argued that Romanticism may have borrowed this idea of culture from the structure of the Middle Ages, which had a conception of cultural life built around the idea of unity. In this respect the attraction which the Middle Ages exerted upon the Romantics was far from accidental but revealed a deep affinity between the two eras. The study of the medieval times during the Romantic period was a good example of how an enquiry into the past can be sympathetically conducted. The Middle Ages had certainly received some attention previously. During the Renaissance the interest in the past was extended to the medieval period too. But this interest was usually the result of contemporary considerations. Either as nostalgia which was trying to find in the past happier times to imitate and bring back, or as an endeavour to establish origins (national, political, ecclesiastical etc.),[39] the past would be used to transport almost anything other than its own real stories into the present. It has been stressed that the "mentality of that period was increasingly ahistorical" and it would remain so until the later Enlightenment.[40] While the Renaissance did not really like or understand the Middles Ages and the Enlightenment positively despised them, Romanticism was fascinated by that period and tried to dispel the popular view that "the Middle Ages represented a period of darkness when man was kept tongue-tied by authority."[41]

The medieval period epitomised a cultural formation that was gradually coming under attack in the post medieval realities. Its message was almost extinct, but it was a message distinctly different. Against a fragmented life that was actively and theoretically encouraged and pursued from the Renaissance on, the medieval period offered one of unity of the life of the spirit. An apt characterisation had been provided by R.G. Collingwood, who in *Speculum Mentis*, called attention to this feature of the Middle Ages, the "unity of the mind, the interdependence of all these interests"[42] our lives are composed of, art, religion, philosophy and so forth. This may give the impression that the medieval mind was not particularly free, especially compared with that of the Renaissance when freedom was understood as "freedom for all the different activities of the mind from interference by each other."[43] But the Middle Ages too had their own, peculiar freedom, "the freedom of occupying an ordained place which one desires to occupy and finds happiness in occupying. This is a freedom in which there is no conflict, a positive freedom, like the freedom of a child at play."[44] Collingwood contrasts this with the freedom of the Renaissance, where one may leave that ordained place and begin to wander. But this freedom creates an internal conflict "between the self that wants to wander and the self that wants to stay at home."[45] Thus the freedom of the Renaissance is a negative freedom, "the freedom to outrage one's own nature."[46]

The Middle Ages seem to have achieved a curious and unsentimental equilibrium that was missing from almost all successive periods. The medieval sense of freedom, a more domesticated and tame freedom, may appear to be in conflict with a wild and unsettled Romanticism. But it is at this point that the strange affection of the Romantics for the medieval times begins to make more sense. The historical spirit of Romanticism is the spirit of belonging. Romanticism may seem, at times, unrestrained but deep down was a spiritual quest for tranquillity, familiarity, and rootedness, those qualities which constitute a well-grounded and well-examined life. The freedom to occupy an "ordained place" is the realisation that we occupy a specific place in the historical process which is a contingent and an ephemeral place, but also ours. The real sense of freedom comes from the appreciation that from this specific, historical position we already have enough to begin building our lives and producing a meaningful image of our experience. This is how the unity of the mind or the unity of a culture may be understood: as the special form, out of the very many potential forms, that life and experience took for us. This unity will be broken and the special form will become bewildered if we begin to think in abstract terms of ideal forms instead of trusting our own concrete, historical experience. One of the problems with the Renaissance, and subsequent, forms of life and freedom was that they were in need of comparison to discover purer forms. Imitating the past, finding solace in things which other people have done, would cast doubt on the present. Despising the past was also a form of comparison, the elevation and praise of the present. But why would the present require such validation if not because it could not itself produce convincing forms of life and freedom? It would be unfair to consider those forms inadequate or incomplete just because they had not attained something more real and deep. A culture became incomprehensible as a unity because its constituents had to assume ideal forms, and ideal forms should transcend historical types. It was a constant and uneasy quest. Behind the confident images of the Renaissance and the Enlightenment the loss of balance frequently loomed: somewhere, something else and something better exists. But the self who wants to wander sometimes gets lost, progress may be another name for this fruitless wandering.

With regard to myths, the Romantic idea of cultural unity suggests that they could be studied more profitably when seen as an integral part of the cultural system of the societies that produced and used them. Myth seeing as a-historical concepts had often given the impression that could be explained as archetypes, images, symbols, structures or, even worse, as recurring errors of certain modes of thinking. Regarded, however, as parts of a wider cultural environment myths invite anyone to study them in terms of how they supported that cultural reality. It may be said that understanding the concept of culture as possessing a unity adds something mysterious and enigmatic to it. It also implies that many of the inner workings of any given culture remain impalpable to the outsiders, and are ultimately comprehensible only to the cultural participants themselves. The latter point seems, to a certain extent, to be true and the main reason why different cultures exercise a certain fascination to outsiders. They owe their attractiveness and their allure precisely to the fact that they are only partially understood and a portion of them remains indecipherable. The moment we think that we have decoded all the symbols and themes of a culture this is when its spell lessens or vanishes altogether. Although a total decipherment of a culture may not be possible, it could still yield enough when considered as an attempt to decrease the chaotic character of our experience by arranging our ideas and principles around a common purpose.

The emergence of Romanticism: the relationship between history and political philosophy

Romanticism emerged as a longing for order, balance and equilibrium. This is what it had requested through its historical spirit, by considering things such as historical process, historical change, culture, and tradition. The same could be requested by way of its political assumptions, looking closely at what binds human societies together and what are the political and social assumptions for achieving and sustaining it. This was not a different set of questions, political as opposed to historical. In Romanticism political concepts are in effect historical concepts, in the sense that they owe their existence to the acknowledgment of human societies as products of a complex, developmental process and not the creation of a rootless, abstract theorising. The details of the exact relationship between the political theory and the historiography of Romanticism and the precise direction of influences need not concern us here. We could only sketch some basic outlines of how the two main political cultures were shaped, how history has influenced political theory and how the two areas may be bridged in the writings of certain Romantic thinkers ideally situated to do so.

* * *

The historical appearance of Romanticism as a new historical consciousness has often been seen in the wider context of a response against the excesses of the French Revolution and some of the assumptions of the Enlightenment. The tremors of radical change often fail to overthrow and instead stimulate a firmer hold over the old and the familiar. The Enlightenment and the French Revolution, however, were for the most part successful in achieving what they set out to achieve, upsetting the existing structures and premises of old Europe. Although it was not a mere response to contemporary historical events, Romanticism viewed under this light is indeed partly reactionary in having to counterbalance certain aspirations of the incoming new order. But its reaction was of a particular kind, as it did not necessarily oppose reform as such. It reacted both against the violent manner and the carelessness of the imposed changes, and also against the content of the changes which were at variance with any serious and honest engagement with the past.

At the level of political philosophy Romanticism articulated common beliefs of the pre Revolutionary period which, although to some degree entrenched, had remained unexpressed in terms of social and political theory. They had also remained largely unexamined, not clearly responding to a gradual post medieval decline of the structures which were holding those beliefs together. To the contrary, the French Revolution actively helped to vocalise the new political awareness as a different political discourse, a specific way to think about political problems. This did stimulate a certain excitement, although in a sense it is still uncertain whether the new awareness has done much to clarify the realm of theoretical politics. The new political categories seemed to belong to a limited spectrum of possibilities. Many of the medieval and post medieval nuances and complexities would be forced to dissolve into artificially constructed opposites, and the new categories would succeed in cultivating more rigid political and cultural spheres which at times led to an oversimplification not only of social life but of reality as well. In this respect it is very doubtful whether the political philosophy of Romanticism, for all its engagement with the post revolutionary realities and its responses to the new challenges, actually adopted any of the new categories of interpretation and analysis. The political lineage of Romanticism had more in common with pre modern modes of analysis and its political language and preoccupations remained rooted in historical terms, trying to make sense of what was left of the medieval order in Europe. The entire social and political activity could only be understood in historical terms. As the slow and complicated development of institutions and practices. Here again history and not theory is the guiding principle: the imperfections of the tested may be fixed, but the untried and the arbitrary theoretical novelties may easily lead to unscrupulous promises and exploitation. Delicate, even fragile, certainties are to be preferred to mere possibilities.

Previously it was due to the balance of the various centres of authority that the basic structural unity and stability was achieved and provided points of reference or meaning for a society to win coherence. Within these structures the peculiar but surprisingly lasting medieval freedom allowed the pursuit of individual activity to occur almost unhindered by unnecessary interferences. In sharp contrast with what came afterwards, what held that social arrangement together was a workable distribution of responsibilities between the various centres of authority, the medieval "story of freedom is one of institutions and laws which balanced the demands of the dominant powers in these small societies."[47] These structures were successful, and ultimately meaningful too, not because they were correct in all their details but because they were historically tried, the product of a complicated and long experiment. Their longevity is telling, and it has been argued that "[t]here is much to be said for the view that the thousand years between the fall of the Roman empire and the emergence of the modern world is the most important strand of all in the weaving of our political texture."[48]

In place of traditional institutions, recognised centres of authority and historical allegiances, the post revolutionary vocabulary erected abstract notions of social arrangements that owed very little to a developmental process by which societies had reached – however imperfectly – the specific historical point they had. The new bureaucracies favoured politics as an activity which emanates from a rather restricted number of sources. The "political" now gradually came to mean not a negotiable and flexible – and necessarily imprecise – affair, taking place within the wider circumstances of a society (which had been more of a medieval practice than a feature of the modern period) but a centrally organised strategy, almost an ideal, dominated by a piecemeal detachment from established practices. There was a renewed emphasis on the individual who now is abstracted from current concerns and historical settings. Chained to ideas of progress and perfection the individual ceases to be a concrete reality and becomes a vision to be attained, or a frail artefact to be protected by a utopian perimeter. An uneasy relationship emerges, therefore, between the creation of constant requirements and demands to shape the new vision, and the necessary conditions to fulfil them. In that sense it may not be a great paradox that the modern conception of politics, with the individual as the centrepiece, did not really believe that personal freedom and responsibility could be the main incentives for individual action. It progressively built a vast state apparatus and great many ancillary institutions to manage, serve and very often curtail that individual. It is also one of the prominent characteristics of the new political realities that there was a stronger concern with influencing the actual content of the social relationships instead of describing or delineating their basic features. The discussion often seemed to involve not just the preconditions of political and social life but some of the outcomes that such preconditions may or should aspire to. It was also thought that these political aspirations were within the purview of the new bureaucratic structure, to be supported or even imposed by it based largely on unprecedented and untried ideas. A period of abstraction had been inaugurated in political life.

These two political cultures would exist side by side but they would differ substantially in almost all respects. Their language, their point of origin, their presumptions and their actual goals would often give the impression that they do not address common problems from different perspectives, but offer competing alternatives on issues of social organisation and even life itself. In a sense the various transformations of these two basic political cultures still retain this legacy of truncated communication, but the overall differences appear better hidden.

Notes

1 Haddock, *Introduction to Historical Thought*, 104-5; Bentley, *Modern Historiography*, 26.
2 Feldman and Richardson, *Rise of Modern Mythology*, 165.
3 Vico, *Autobiography*, 153.
4 Berlin, *Vico and Herder*, 72.
5 Hughes, *Consciousness and Society*, 208.
6 Bentley, *Modern Historiography*, 26.
7 Barzun, *From Dawn to Decadence*, 465.
8 Ibid., 466.
9 Ibid., 465.
10 Berlin, *Sense of Reality*, 168.
11 Ibid., 170.
12 Berlin, *Roots of Romanticism*, 1.
13 Scruton, *From Descartes to Wittgenstein*, 138.
14 Ibid., 164.
15 Barzun, *From Dawn to Decadence*, 466.
16 See for instance various definitions in Berlin, *Roots of Romanticism*, 14-16; also Barzun, "Intrinsic and Historic Romanticism," 18-29; and Barzun, *Classic, Romantic and Modern*, 155-68.

17 Berlin, *Roots of Romanticism*, 8.
18 Collingwood, *Idea of History*, 86.
19 Ibid., 87.
20 Ibid., 88.
21 Ibid.
22 Croce, "Crisis of Faith," 53.
23 Vincent, *History*, 123.
24 Becker, *The Heavenly City*, 93.
25 Ibid., 94.
26 Trevor-Roper, *Romantic Movement, 9.*
27 Ibid., 23.
28 Bentley, *Modern Historiography*, 24.
29 Croce, "Crisis of Faith," 53.
30 Bentley, *Modern Historiography*, 26.
31 Collingwood, *Idea of History*, 210.
32 Butterfield, *Whig Interpretation of History*, 9.
33 Collingwood, *Idea of History*, 154.
34 Berlin, *Against the Current*, 101.
35 Scruton, *Green Philosophy*, 321.
36 Minogue, *Politics*, 48.
37 Ibid.
38 Scruton, *Green Philosophy*, 321.
39 Bouwsma, *The Waning of the Renaissance*, 209-10.
40 Ibid., 214. Bouwsma discusses these ideas in a chapter suggestively called "The Decline of Historical Consciousness."
41 Butterfield, *Whig Interpretation of History*, 13. Butterfield writing in 1931 believed that this view "is still not quite eradicated" (Ibid.)
42 Collingwood, *Speculum Mentis*, 30.
43 Ibid.
44 Ibid.
45 Ibid., 31.
46 Ibid.
47 Minogue, *Politics*, 28.
48 Ibid., 25.

References

Barzun, Jacques. *From Dawn To Decadence. 1500 to the Present: 500 Years of Western Cultural Life.* London: Harper Collins Publishers, 2000.
Barzun, Jacques. *Classic, Romantic and Modern.* 2nd edition. Boston and Toronto: Little, Brown and Co., 1961.
Barzun, Jacques. "Intrinsic and Historic Romanticism." In *Romanticism. Problems of Definition, Explanation, and Evaluation*, edited with an introduction by John B. Halsted, 18–29. Lexington, Massachusetts: D.C. Heath & Company, 1965.
Becker, Carl Lotus. *The Heavenly City of the Eighteenth-Century Philosophers.* New Haven: Yale University Press, 1932.

Bentley, Michael. *Modern Historiography: An Introduction*. London: Routledge, 1999.

Berlin, Isaiah. *Vico and Herder. Two Studies in the History of Ideas*. London: The Hogarth Press, 1976.

Berlin, Isaiah. *Against the Current. Essays in the History of Ideas*, edited and with a bibliography by Henry Hardy, with an introduction by Roger Hausheer. Oxford: Oxford University Press, 1981.

Berlin, Isaiah. *The Roots of Romanticism*, edited by Henry Hardy. Princeton, New Jersey: Princeton University Press, 1999.

Berlin, Isaiah. *The Sense of Reality. Studies in Ideas and Their History*, edited by Henry Hardy, with an introduction by Patrick Gardiner. New York: Farrar, Straus and Giroux, 1997.

Bouwsma, William James. *The Waning of the Renaissance, 1550-1640*. New Haven and London: Yale University Press, 2000.

Butterfield, Herbert. *The Whig Interpretation of History*. London: George Bell and Sons, 1931.

Collingwood, Robin George. *Speculum Mentis or The Map of Knowledge*. Oxford: Oxford University Press, 1924.

Collingwood, Robin George. *The Idea of History*. Oxford: Oxford University Press, 1946 (Revised edition with Lectures 1926-1928, edited with an introduction by Jan van der Dussen, Oxford: Oxford University Press, 1994).

Croce, Benedetto. "A Crisis of Faith." In *Romanticism. Problems of Definition, Explanation, and Evaluation*, edited with an introduction by John B. Halsted, 53–57. Lexington, Massachusetts: D.C. Heath & Company, 1965.

Feldman, Burton and Richardson, Robert D. *The Rise of Modern Mythology, 1680-1860*. Bloomington: Indiana University Press, 1972.

Haddock, Bruce Anthony. *An Introduction to Historical Thought*. London: Edward Arnold Ltd., 1980.

Hughes, Henry Stuart. *Consciousness and Society: The Reorientation of European Social Thought, 1890-1930*. New York: Alfred A. Knopf, 1958.

Minogue, Kenneth. *Politics. A Very Short Introduction*. Oxford: Oxford University Press, 1995.

Scruton, Roger. *From Descartes to Wittgenstein. A short history of modern philosophy*. London: Routledge & Kegan Paul, 1981.

Scruton, Roger. *Green Philosophy. How to Think Seriously About the Planet*. London: Atlantic Books, 2012.

Trevor-Roper, Hugh Redwald. *The Romantic Movement and the Study of History. The John Coffin Memorial Lecture*. London: The Athlone Press, University of London, 1969.

Vico, Giambattista. *The Autobiography of Giambattista Vico*. Translated by Max Harold Fisch and Thomas Goddard Bergin. Ithaca: Cornell University Press, 1944.

Vincent, John. *History*. London: Continuum, 2005 (First published in 1995 by Duckworth as An Intelligent Person's Guide to History).

5 Edmund Burke: the forgotten historian

The significant enlargement of centralised, administrative bureaucracies at the expense of the inherited rights, life, and customs of traditional communities was part of a new, and in various instances insidious, reality. This reality was making clear advances for quite some time mainly through the political discourse of the Enlightenment, but it established itself more securely in the aftermath of the French Revolution. It was a situation which run contrary to the spirit of Romanticism with its emphasis on rather small societies with their own traditional rhythms and intricate historical roots. The alarming implications of these developments had become clear to historians but "they had not yet been elaborated at the level of political philosophy."[1] The atrocities of the French Revolution helped to extend "the historical disposition to the heart of political debate."[2] That things moved from history to theory (political philosophy) is quite important. In so far as the main characteristic of Romanticism was its heightened historical consciousness, the concrete historical situation, and its details would take precedence over abstract theoretical formulations. To answer any question or tackle any problem based on such abstract reasoning would perhaps satisfy many Enlightenment thinkers but for the Romantic thinkers it was essential that any historical argument and analysis would have to come before any philosophical articulation. Otherwise any claim to a strong historical consciousness is invalidated.

Therefore, any suggestions that Romantic historians began to see the past as "the only possible basis for ... political stability" under the influence of political theorists like Edmund Burke,[3] misunderstand the basic relationship between history and political theory by reversing the order of the Romantic interpretation. It is not because of theoretical approaches that the function and the validity of the past are to be understood, but it is the historical appreciation of the past which will provide justification to political theory to elaborate in more abstract

DOI: 10.4324/9781315387703-7

and theoretical terms what the historical reality had already conceived. History supplies political theory with the necessary material to conceptualise but with as little abstraction and generalisation as possible. Eventually both history and political theory will converge and their message would be the same: caution. Caution about the complexities of the past societies, about risky and easy generalisations, about misplaced analogies, about changing and disturbing too much, too quickly, and too irrevocably. Caution creates a bond between the observer and the phenomena, almost a bond of affection which is more difficult to achieve through abstract, theoretical approaches which usually favour detachment. Caution, for history, exemplifies a genuine interest for the past, seeking understanding and knowledge by suspending the immediate demands of the present. For political philosophy caution becomes a guiding precept that places emphasis upon careful analysis and comprehension as opposed to the prescription of remedies for hastily studied and ill understood social situations. The pressure or disdain that such conceptions of history and political philosophy may encounter from several demands for action may give rise to further opportunities for refinement. But the conflict between these positions (caution and action) is not something easily managed as they both set out to discover different aspects of the world.

Certainly the priority of history over theory does not mean that the two can not belong to the same line of enquiry, and it may be argued that the most fruitful work was often carried out by people who combined both identities. There were, indeed, people such as Edmund Burke and Joseph de Maistre who responded, using a recognisably Romantic idiom, to the excesses of unguarded visions of total societal transformation. Their responses were essentially Romantic because of the strong historical undertones that many of their premises and arguments had. With de Maistre, for instance, a historical outlook permeated his thought to the extent that his writing career was "centered on the idea of history."[4] Although his actual historical output is not very substantial, his writings contain "deeply historicizing themes"[5] and it is constantly against a historical background that he explored and formulated his ideas. He called history "experimental politics" and if we turn to it, he argues, we shall see "the cradle of nations surrounded by priests and hear a constant call to God for help in human weakness. Myth, much truer than ancient history for trained eyes, adds to this proof."[6] In fact de Maistre praised myth because he believed it "to be part of divine revelation."[7]

Edmund Burke the political philosopher, the polemicist, the fierce critic of the French Revolution and of some of the philosophical assumptions and justifications which made it possible, is well established. Burke the active politician and the speech maker is invaluable to the student of political history inasmuch as, Lord Acton maintained, "Burke at his best is England at its best."[8] Burke the historian is less well known, although he predates and also moulds Burke the political theorist. He essentially began his writing career as historian. In the post Revolutionary world he was one of the most well suited to explain how the gap between historical reality and political abstraction should be bridged, if normal life is to be pursued. Instead, therefore, of just an influence on Romantic historians, showing them how the past can be the only basis for political stability, he was also the creator of those historical presuppositions which made the political argument possible and viable. The dual aspect of Burke emerges more clearly when his position is aligned with the presuppositions of Romanticism.

Burke is not easy to categorise, he was a "master of rhetorical presentation" and close attention should be paid to his language.[9] For his preference "for the organic (against the manufactured), for instinct (against reason), for the concrete, historical and traditional (against the new, arbitrary, abstract), for the unconscious (against the conscious)" he has been seen as "the father of German political romanticism."[10] Himmelfarb had tried to place him within the English Enlightenment,[11] arguing that he is not usually thought of as one of the romantics.[12] She also saw him as quite influential in the developments of the practice of history, contending that the English Whig historians "including some notably un-Whiggish types" were descending from Burke and Macaulay.[13]

Lord Acton, on the other hand, believed that Burke was behind various aspects of the Romantic movement,[14] that history "issues from the Romantic School ... It hails from Burke."[15] One of his early writings is devoted to Burke's historical qualities and is full of praise. He believed Burke's *The Abridgement of English History* to have been his "most remarkable literary production" and expressed little doubt that "as Burke was our greatest statesman, so he would have been the first of our historians."[16] Lord Acton thought that Burke "was free both from vulgar prejudice and from pedantry; and no other man was so well fitted to adorn history with the attainments of a great scholar."[17] He recognised that Burke's book was atypical for the time it was written (the book was written in 1757 but was not published until 1812, some time after Burke's death) especially with respect to the Middle Ages, a period either vilified or most likely ignored as one of obscurantism and backwardness. Burke spoke "of mediaeval institutions with an intelligence and appreciation which in his time were ... rare" and thus exemplified concrete historical virtues by showing himself "superior to that system of prejudice and ignorance which was then universal."[18]

Croce in his discussion of Bolingbroke argues that he failed to realise the importance of "that primitive barbaric history, which he threw into a corner as useless dead leaves."[19] This history, however, was to reappear "quite fresh half a century later, as the result of the reaction against intellectualism and Jacobinism, and that this reaction would have as one of its principal promoters a publicist of his own country, Burke."[20] Croce put Burke alongside Vico, who had done the same thing sometime earlier. Both of them reacted against prevailing moods and a-historical conceptions of social life, inaugurating a quite new historical attitude. Croce values Burke's involvement in terms of what it did for history, especially pre Renaissance history, which Bolingbroke considered essentially untrue and dead.

For Butterfield the study of the past became more profound through "the right imaginative approach—the cultivation of what we call historical-mindedness ... almost a new dimension added to our thinking."[21] Although there was "a remarkable lack of it in the Renaissance and even in much of the eighteenth century", signs of this attitude were present in some seventeenth century English writers, in Vico, in Herder, and even in some overlooked achievements during the eighteenth century.[22] But for Butterfield it was really Edmund Burke "who –having recovered contact with the historical achievements of Restoration England– exerted the presiding influence over the historical movement of the nineteenth century."[23] Burke's *Abridgement*, Butterfield continues, is significant "in view of its place in the chronological series"[24] and it is perhaps not always quite apparent to the students of Burke's thought "to what a degree the historical views which it embodies must actually entail the characteristic features of the man's political outlook."[25]

Meinecke in tracing the rise and development of the new historical outlook of Historicism (or "Historism") devoted a substantial discussion on Burke, almost twice as long as that on Gibbon. Burke is considered a part of the pre-Romantic movement, "a figure of European importance who had a lasting influence on historical thought in the future."[26] The *Abridgement* was a book that "revealed the stirrings of a new historical sense that went beyond anything Hume had written under the influence of the Enlightenment."[27] In sharp contrast with the Enlightenment, Meinecke sees in Burke's treatment of the Middle Ages no condemnation whatsoever but a "deep inner feeling of the continuity in life, and the oneness of past and present."[28] Throughout the book Burke is respectful of the achievements of religion, and although he would in essence disagree with how ancient people understood religion his judgement was rather balanced and fair:

> but it must be owned that in general their ideas [i.e., the Druids] of divine matters were more exalted that those of the Greeks and Romans; and that they did not fall into an idolatry so coarse and vulgar. That their gods should be represented under a human form, they thought derogatory to beings uncreated and imperishable. To confine what can endure no limits within walls and roofs, they judged absurd and impious. In these particulars there was something refined, and suitable enough to a just idea of the Divinity.[29]

That primitive people were thus disposed was not surprising as Burke characteristically maintained that the "first openings of civility have been everywhere made by religion."[30] For Meinecke Burke's historical sense is most clearly illustrated by his feeling "for all that is institutional in the past, seeing in it the roots of our modern institutions, and for the way that it has gradually risen to a higher stage from very rough and obscure beginnings."[31] Burke, thus, is aware of the developmental character of history and the continuity between past and present.

While Meinecke's discussion in general is quite penetrating, his choice to include various thinkers as historicism's forerunners has been criticised because, allegedly, many of them such as "Shaftesbury, Leibniz, Gottfried Arnold, Vico, Montesquieu, and the 'pre-Romantic' Burke, were not historians."[32] It was thought they were only included because they exemplified in various degrees the two attributes of historicism which Meinecke considered important, namely the idea of individuality and the idea of development.[33] It is not quite clear what is the reason for this idiosyncratic denial of the status of historian to these people. Whether it rests on definitional technicalities or expectations of what a historian is or should be, shaped by the subsequent professionalisation of history (in which case almost every pre nineteenth century historian would not be considered a historian), there is little doubt that most of the people Meinecke mentions had a good claim to be included as historians of some description. In so far as many of them were pursuing methodological issues or enquiries into the epistemological value of history, their work would belong, sure enough, to a more philosophical type of history. Often, however, their work combined coherently and convincingly the abstract and the empirical, advancing philosophical considerations alongside more conventionally understood historical material. Their work occupied this approximate region between history and philosophy and whether this type of history should be open to more objections and resistance due to its broader aspirations, this is an altogether different issue. They may have been too ambitious or too enterprising historians but they were certainly dealing with genuine historical problems.

It is partly because of such idiosyncratic opinions that the fate of various thinkers is sometimes decided. Burke could all too easily be dismissed as irrelevant during a period when historical concerns were beginning to move to a different direction; or because he did not write a work of pure historical character in later life; or because he was an uncomfortable advocate of things that the new historical developments assumed had surpassed and rendered outdated. Although hardly justifiable from the point of view of the history of historical thought, all these things would at least, in some measure, explain this silent ostracism and Burke's obscurity as historian and as historical innovator. The historical dimension of Burke may remain forgotten or ignored, bypassed or unnoticed, but at the expense of nuances, historical accuracy, and historical depth. For the fact remains that his political pronouncements and writings were always anchored to historical circumstance and not abstract theoretical principles.

It would also be a mistake to see Burke as "drawing on the commonplaces of the *ars historica* tradition"[34] and conceiving history as a teacher and reservoir of lessons from the past to guide our present and future actions. If things are strongly influenced by historical circumstances it means that it can not be easy to transpose lessons from one historical period to another. For Romanticism, and thus for Burke also, the past is unique, it should be seen in its own terms, with each period having a special character and exhibiting certain attitudes and features individual enough to render them unsuitable and unusable as general lessons. But most importantly the past is linked with individual traditions that represent a continuity to be respected for its complexity and durability. We can not precisely say how societies came to be what they are, how the myriad factors have contributed to create a certain structure which is labyrinthine and without clear historical antecedent. Any lessons, therefore, that may come from a certain society and a certain tradition will at best be applicable to subsequent stages of the same society only. But even within a certain tradition these lessons are nothing more than a basic reluctance to advocate radical change. If Burke could ever be tempted to place history in the service of instruction it would be to offer not a lesson as such but a warning, perhaps permeated by a general pessimism. The free agency of human will makes it impossible to predict the forms that human ingenuity and benevolence may take, but for the same reason human fear and frailty are constantly tempted to evade the burden of responsibility. It was more than anything else Burke's emphasis on the evils in human actions, amplified by the recent events of the French Revolution and the introduction of new and unprecedented cruelties.

Burke's forgotten contribution to the shaping of a new historical consciousness is also a forgotten chapter in the history of Romantic historiography and a partially explored aspect of his political thought. In historiographical terms he exemplified the Romantic attitude by his "deep engagement and sympathy with the cultures under examination"[35] and by his attention to broader concerns of culture and civilisation, such as customs, law, and religious ideas, alongside political history and institutions. Moreover, any understanding of his political ideas and responses will be incomplete without a clear grasp that they rest on premises responsive to historical modes of thinking.

Notes

1 Haddock, *Introduction to Historical Thought*, 100.
2 Ibid.
3 Evans, *In Defence of History*, 16.
4 Armenteros, *French Idea of History*, 2.
5 Ibid., 3.
6 Lively, *de Maistre*, 162.
7 Ibid., 31.
8 Lord Acton, *Lectures on Modern History*, 261.
9 Haddock, *History of Political Thought*, 189.
10 Heer, *Intellectual History of Europe*, 379.
11 Himmelfarb, *Roads to Modernity*, 71–92 (mainly Section 3. Edmund Burke's Enlightenment).
12 Ibid., 137.
13 Himmelfarb, *New History and Old*, 3. See also 143–8 for a contrast between Burke and Macaulay.
14 Butterfield, *Man on his Past*, 68.
15 Quoted in ibid., 70.
16 Lord Acton, *Essays on Church and State*, 455.
17 Ibid., 456.
18 Ibid., 455.
19 Croce, *Historiography*, 31.
20 Ibid.
21 Butterfield, *Man on his Past*, 17.
22 Ibid., 17–8.
23 Ibid., 18.
24 Ibid., 68.
25 Ibid., 69.
26 Meinecke, *Historism*, 219.

27 Ibid., 221.
28 Ibid., 231.
29 Burke, *Works*, 201.
30 Ibid., 196.
31 Meinecke, *Historism*, 221.
32 Kelley, *Faces of History*, 266.
33 Ibid.
34 Ibid., 257.
35 Norman, *Edmund Burke*, 32.

References

Armenteros, Carolina. 2011. *The French Idea of History. Joseph de Maistre and his Heirs, 1794–1854*. Ithaca and London: Cornell University Press, 2011.

Burke, Edmund. *The Works of Edmund Burke. Vol. VI*. London: George Bell and Sons, 1894.

Butterfield, Herbert. *Man on His Past. The Study of the History of Historical Scholarship*. Cambridge: Cambridge University Press, 1955.

Croce, Benedetto. *Theory and History of Historiography*. Translated by Douglas Ainslie. London: George G. Harrap & Co. Ltd, 1921.

Evans, Richard John. *In Defence of History*. London: Granta Books, 1997.

Haddock, Bruce Anthony. *An Introduction to Historical Thought*. London: Edward Arnold Ltd., 1980.

Haddock, Bruce Anthony. *A History of Political Thought. From Antiquity to the Present*. Cambridge: Polity Press, 2008.

Heer, Friedrich. *The Intellectual History of Europe*. Translated by Jonathan Steinberg. Cleveland and New York: The World Publishing Company, 1966.

Himmelfarb, Gertrude. *The New History and the Old*. Cambridge, Massachusetts: The Belknap Press of Harvard University Press, 1987.

Himmelfarb, Gertrude. *The Roads to Modernity. The British, French, and American Enlightenments*. New York: Alfred A. Knopf, 2004.

Kelley, Donald R. *Faces of History. Historical Inquiry From Herodotus to Herder*. New Haven and London: Yale University Press, 1998.

Lively, Jack. *The Works of Joseph de Maistre*. Selected, translated and introduced by Jack Lively. New Forward by Robert Nisbet. New York: Schocken Books, 1971.

Lord Acton. *Essays on Church and State*. Edited and introduced by Douglas Woodruff. London: Hollis and Carter, 1952.

Lord Acton. *Lectures on Modern History*. With an introduction by Hugh Trevor-Roper. London: Fontana/Collins, 1960.

Meinecke, Friedrich. *Historism. The Rise of a New Historical Outlook*. Translated by J.E. Anderson. London: Routledge & Kegan Paul Ltd, 1972.

Norman, Jesse. *Edmund Burke. The Visionary Who Invented Modern Politics*. London: William Collins, 2013.

The historicity of myths: some thoughts on history and myth

With myth's historical sense there is frequently a feeling that something still lingers on from the past, neither as yet settled nor quite apprehended, which refuses to go away. Myth is there, taciturn, unyielding, Sibylline. Croce, for instance, maintained that the thought of the first historians or "logographs," and the thought of Herodotus "really does unite itself with religions, myths, theogonies, cosmogonies, genealogies, and with legendary and epical tales, which were not indeed poetry, or were not only poetry but also thoughts—that is to say, metaphysics and histories."[1] Jaspers, again, argued that when the Mythical Age "with its tranquillity and self-evidence" was defeated by *logos*, myth "became the material of a language which expressed by it something very different from what it had originally signified: it was turned into parable."[2] The contrast between myth as parable and myth as originally something very different, is very much like the contrast between truth and falsehood. This is, at least, what must have looked like to the "mass of the people" who continued to believe in myth even after it had been destroyed and the "old mythical world slowly sank into oblivion."[3] What myth came to "stand for," fables, allegorical stories, and ostensible histories invented by Euhemerus, would mean nothing to societies that had accepted myths. For those societies myth was "a true story of what had befallen them; a story growing out of the encounter with the holy; a story which manifests the true nature of the world, and which is therefore the basis for relating oneself and one's society to the world."[4] In other words, myth is a form of explanation and understanding of human experience and reality. Let us endeavour to unravel this characterisation of myth a bit further to see if we can establish more certainty about it.

By saying that myths, or some myths, may imply a historical possibility we may be referring to two distinct, but quite easy to confuse, things. The first would be to say that by examining myths we need not

DOI: 10.4324/9781315387703-8

concern ourselves with whether they furnish us with facts or fables, with truth or with entirely fictitious stories and legends. Instead our enquiry will have to consider them as documents which reveal something about the people who created them, their mentality, their manners, their concerns, and the working of their minds in some general sense. This is indeed a very plausible and legitimate line of enquiry. But it may seem that by treating or using myths in this way we are not so much concerned with their content but with their general form as manifestations or expressions of a certain age and of a certain group of people. Thus, it may also be tempting to say that we are not necessarily doing something substantially different by examining myths as opposed to any other form of expression. Myths examined in such a way would be historical only in the wider sense of detecting the human spirit expressing, so to speak, itself in different ways under certain historical conditions. But this is not exactly so because the question is not only what it means for societies to have used myths, but also why the mythical narrative took the specific form it took. The form of the narrative differentiates myth from other narratives and activities and gives it specific features that may indicate a closer connection with history. In fact this, as we shall see, appears to be true: the form of myth is linked decisively with history, both are ways of selecting, ordering, and organising the available material in order to understand experience and reality.

The second thing we may imply by referring to the historical possibility of myths, would be to ask a rather clear question about their content. Are myths, or at least some classes of myths, primarily a type of narrative of something that approximates truth? In the way that Vico is thought to have understood myth as "a story in which is expressed the way in which man encounters, understands, and interacts with his world."[5] Vico had approached mythology and etymology trying to find their original meaning. He though that the "definition of Μύθος ... is 'a true narration', yet it survived with the meaning of the word 'fable', which everyone has hitherto taken to mean a false narration."[6] Using this definition to study ancient myths he tried to demonstrate that "mythologies ... are histories of facts"[7] and the fables "were true and trustworthy histories of the customs of the most ancient peoples of Greece."[8] With etymology he also thinks that a corrupted meaning has prevailed as the "definition of Έτυμον ... is 'true speech'. In the vulgar it means 'origin' or 'history of words'."[9] In the end Vico believed he had discovered new principles of mythology and etymology showing that "fables and true speech were one and the same in meaning and that they constituted the vocabulary of the first nations"[10] and that "all the histories of the gentiles have their beginnings in fables, which were the first histories of the gentile nations."[11] Although initially trustworthy, time obscured the real meaning of those myths and fables and this is how they came down to us, Vico argues.[12] Even great theorists like Grotius, Selden and Pufendorf, because they lacked a proper critical method, did not realise that myths and fables could be interpreted as sources for reconstructing the life of the early people.[13]

In reality the aforementioned two ways to see myths, the form and the content of the narrative, can not be separated. To say that something has form and content is not particularly insightful as the two things are not really separate in any meaningful way. To believe that they are has often led to misunderstandings, in believing, for example, that it is possible to examine the structure of myths without any reference to the content of the stories themselves. But there is a sense in which these two concepts may be of help: when we contrast myth with history. Assuming that history and myth perform similar but not identical functions, anatomise them more closely may help us determine the approximate boundaries of each. In doing so we will be able to see more clearly the historical function of myth.

What is, then, the relationship between history and myth? What do we mean when we refer to the historicity of myths? One explanation has it that "history is basically a mythic way of perceiving the world" and those who believe such a thing "affirm that reality is historical in nature"[14] History, the argument goes, "is a way of perceiving and ordering the totality of human experience in which ultimate or sacral meaning is understood to be present in empirical and transitory phenomena."[15] Understanding reality historically means the attempt to understand primarily man himself and phenomena created by man, but also every other area of human experience, including nature.[16] History is thus all encompassing, it offers "a comprehensive intellectual and social organization of the world ... [and] the 'true story' of how the world is and is to be perceived."[17] Likewise, the argument continues, myth serves the same function, its "essential aspects" being the characteristics we also find in history, namely a "true story about the sacral power which invests man and the world" and that this story makes it possible for us to "perceive and organize all realms of our experience".[18]

This interpretation is suggestive in at least two ways. The first is the recognition that both history and myth offer a truthful story of how things are. Although it is conceded that their truth "cannot be argued conclusively"[19] (as probably is the case with most ultimate explanations of reality), we may expect that any connection between myth and various symbolic, allegorical interpretations (dominant and wide spread as they may be) has been severed. Instead of fanciful stories, primitive attempts at science, and so forth, myths have been rehabilitated as vehicles of a robust explanation of reality, human experience, and the cosmos. History too is regarded as offering a valid view of reality and the world. In a sense this is a continuation of the line initiated with Vico. A line that was to challenge the dominance of the scientific realm as an all embracing mode of explanation. In fact what we are offered now may even be wider, because history is seen as an account of the whole reality as such. Thus this "widening" involves not only a reluctance to accept science as being able to discuss meaningfully man and his creations, but it also elevates history to a position of judging and comprehending nature, at least so far as nature relates to human experience.

(The suggestion that reality and nature are deep down historical is an intriguing feature of history's response to the catholic claims of science. One of the most audacious such suggestions, and rather provocative as well, has been R.G. Collingwood's formulation in *The Idea of Nature*. Arguing against positivism's claims, Collingwood maintained that natural science is not the sole department of human thought and not even a self-sufficient and self-contained form of thought in its dependence "for its very existence" upon another form of thought, which is different from natural science and not reducible to it.[20] Using just natural science is thus inadequate if we wish to answer the question what nature is. To do so we would have to take into account the other form of thought upon which nature and natural science depend. Surprisingly for a scientific minded person, and also unsurprisingly given Collingwood's leanings, this other form of thought is History. He tried to show that "a 'scientific fact' is a class of historical facts" and that the same applies to scientific theories.[21] Thus the historical context and the knowledge of what history is, are indispensable to anyone who wants to understand natural science and to answer what nature is.)

The second way that the interpretation is suggestive has to do with the fact that the story also provides meaning. That is, the story is not only a truthful description and explanation of reality but it offers a very practical aspect too, that of organising our lives according to the story's ultimate meaning. History and myths are related, almost identified with each other, as they perform the same function, providing a story of how reality is and arranging our lives according to the main precepts of this story. As the main argument was effectively trying to link history and myths with theological concerns, this meaning is expressed in divine, sacred, or transcendent terms. Perhaps even with those theological concerns aside we can still see a suggestive, relatively generic, argument for the historicity of myths, a historicity without the ultimate meaning deriving from a sacred source. The sacred meaning, however, is what makes the stories that myth and history offer compelling to follow. A different meaning may have not created a story equally powerful. In the case of myth, moreover, the attachment to religion had always been a recognisable bond and any mythical explanation of ultimate meaning would be expressible in sacred and divine terms. On the other hand the religious character is not often recognised as a necessary element of any historical explanation and history in general shrinks from narratives revealing plans, ultimate purposes or teleological undertones. Metaphysical meanings and speculative philosophies of history may attempt to complete and augment an 'abbreviated' narrative that lacks beginnings and has no conclusion. The uncertainty of how things may have started and how they may end is what makes any such speculative explanations difficult to refute conclusively. A historical narrative, however, with no beginning and no end may still offer a compelling account of the historical process, and while the possibility of an ultimate meaning enhances the narrative's explanatory force, it does not necessarily explain the narrative or interfere with its development. A historical narrative remains faithful to the facts while accepting that a further metaphysics is conceivable, if not inescapable too.

With this qualification in mind it may be said that the argument of history and myth as having a very similar function does elucidate a relationship between the two, with some convincing and interesting features. The most interesting of these features is that history and myth are both stories that explain fundamental things about human experience and the world. As McNeill put it rather succinctly, myth and history "are close kin inasmuch as both explain how things got to be the way they are by telling some sort of story. But our common parlance reckons myth to be false while history is, or aspires to be, true."[22] Our common parlance also reveals another fundamental issue. That those two things that were so close together came to be so different, one narrative came to be seen as truthful while the other was pushed to the opposite end to accompany varieties of falsehood.

If myth and history are so similar we would need to explain why two distinct enquiries, claiming roughly the same function, have existed side-by-side. What unites myth and history, how can we explain their kinship? For one thing to see history as having such a wide purview, to explain and organise human experience and reality, is not without problems. Any stories that history tells are not general but specific and particular. History organises episodes, events, actions, etc. but not the entire human experience as such. Conceivably mythical stories may assume this wider explanatory scope, but even this is debatable. Because, like history, myth too offers stories of concrete and specific events, that took place at a certain time and involved certain people. But there is indeed a sense in which both myth and history may have a broader scope. By facing the undifferentiated mass of experience, all the occurrences, happenings, actions etc., any meaningful narrative will have to begin by a process of rearrangement. It will select and exclude some elements, it will emphasise or downplay certain features. This is a somehow artificial process and as Oakeshott had put it "Classification is a modification of experience and not the concrete whole; it is an arrest in experience."[23] But it seems necessary if we want to bring some order to this seemingly chaotic situation. In so far as both history and myth were involved in classifying experience and reality, they were similar. These structural similarities were already recognised in antiquity in the coexistence, comparison, and occasional tension, between history and myth. Any tension could only exist if the two things in question were in some way competing with each other. This tension was also indicative of the fact that the two areas were in some way distinct and the possibility that history could be absorbed by, or transformed into, myth or myth by history was indeed very slim: the two areas could remain distinct. But this tension was frequently unable to delineate clearer boundaries between the two.

A possible reason why this was the case may be found in that history and myth were somehow related at some point in their early life. Not in a very conscious way but in a way that activities may be related to each other. Activities often arise without clear intentions out of pure curiosity, they may be unplanned and unpremeditated. They may be vaguely aware of their immaturity, they will lack urgency and there will be a sense of innocence about them. The desire to be linked to something 'practical' may not yet be present and thus they may be willing to sacrifice proper judgement and anticipation of outcomes for the pure enjoyment of the activity itself. They may also emerge "naively, like games that children invent for themselves."[24] No activity, for instance, could begin with the clear purpose of describing and explaining experience and also be aware of performing a task which is so specific and distinct from other tasks. It is more likely that confronted with the magnitude and complexity of reality, activities attach themselves to a small corner of this reality and make their own way from there towards something that only gradually becomes more clear. Activities may emerge in this haphazard manner but if they are to remain genuine they will have to become more focused, specialised, and conscious. But because of the contingencies of their emergence, there is no certain way to ensure that different activities will not coincide, clash or overlap with each other. They may do so in various ways. One activity, for instance, may come and find another already there, occupying the same notional space and doing pretty much the same thing. As early activities they will not be fully conscious of their exact identity as yet but if they believe they are vaguely similar they will compete with each other. To merge would also be possible but it rarely happens as one activity would have to be absorbed by the other and their similarities will never be so absolute as to allow this to happen. Thus they will compete for supremacy and their success in performing the similar task they believe they are meant to be performing will decide which activity will survive and which will become obsolete. Such an outcome also rarely happens, for it is difficult accepting defeat for something that has no clear rules of how this competition is to be decided. After all we are talking about activities that emerge to describe and explain a domain which in essence will also be created by these activities by the same process of description and explanation. In raw and unclassified experience there are no boundaries and neatly allocated spaces for specific activities. This does not mean that creation and existence is the same thing, but the main task of any serious activity is to give some shape to the raw material of experience. To go back to how activities may coincide, clash or overlap. Another way would be for different activities to be seen as stages of the same activity as it develops, transforms or evolves over time. As no such transformation is ever quite complete, the various stages of the activity may in fact coexist as different activities, instead of one entirely replacing the other. Both harmony and conflict will characterise the relationship of these activities: harmony on account of their common ambit, conflict in trying one activity to establish its legitimacy over the other. In effect the given two ways – and possibly others too – are not distinct alternatives but they interact with each other until a more certain identity of an activity is formed.

The aforementioned discussion may sound vague and a bit mystical but it is an exceedingly ordinary process, and what in actual fact appears to have happened with many activities. Both competition and transformation may explain the emergence and the subsequent fate of, for instance, alchemy and chemistry, of astrology and astronomy, or antiquarianism and archaeology and so on. In some ways one activity has replaced another, but in some other ways the activities remain distinct and separate. This is a schematic way of how activities emerge, how they become distinct, or even refuse to do so, and thus how their boundaries are often not so very perfectly delineated. This is also a very approximate way to account for the relationship between myth and history and the tendency to see them as having something in common. Understanding their exact relationship is not possible because it would require us to go back to the very origins of things. The purity of such a quest is unattainable. Even without this original certainty, however, we may reasonable say that history and myth were closely related activities. They were charged with describing the picture of reality, experience, and society and its past, and they did so by narrating stories. But similar as they were as activities they also differed.

The necessity, desire or temptation to contrast two activities only arise later on in their lives, when their identities are more fully formed. To contrast activities earlier on, at some notional beginning of their existence, would be impracticable. Either their identities will not be fully formed yet and thus the contrast premature; or their identities will be already very distinct and the need to contrast them does not arise at all. To say, therefore, at some later point of the life of myth and history, that history is, as we have seen previously, "a mythic way of perceiving the world", and that "myth-making represents ... an early and by no means unsubtle attempt at historical thinking"[25] would imply that we reasonably know what myth and history are. It also implies that the contrast is necessary or desirable because of some underlying similarity which both retain from their earlier lives. Why else would we want to contrast the two? Myth and history seem indeed to have begun as stories that tried to explain things in a more or less catholic way. They would describe what has happened, explain why it has happened, and also assign some kind of ultimate meaning to any past, and often present, actions and occurrences. Actions and occurrences to be taken in the wide sense of experience, to include reality and the place of man within it. To a larger extent myth retained this function. History gradually, only gradually, became less ambitious and its new function was thought to be only that of describing and explaining the human past. This much more modest function had left behind the task of describing and explaining experience in general, and also the task of assigning ultimate meaning to both human actions and the wider reality. That this was a gradual process can be seen from the fact that at least some versions of history until the Middle Ages – and in some respects afterwards too – were still trying to explain things in a more comprehensive way, by reference to a historical framework which happily included periods of non recorded history. Eventually even myth lost its broad explanatory power but it happened much later than history and in a completely different way. When it happened it signalled the degeneration of myth and its association with falsehood and allegories. Paradoxically the opposite happened to history. We tend to think that this new, condensed function of history was a wise move away from grand metaphysical explanations towards the elucidation of the factual and the concrete. In this sense, and this sense alone, when myth is regarded in its later, clumsy form, the claim that history should not be myth may be believed.

From these vicissitudes and transformations of the historical and the mythical activities their entire later history may be explained. The contrast between the two is justified because of their early similarity and because their subsequent differences can not possible eliminate this fundamental similarity. The main difference between history and myth became the breadth of their understanding and explanation. Myth would encompass the entire experience, while history would mainly limit itself to understanding and explaining human past actions. As history's remit is part of the wider experience, it would overlap with the mythical story. But history can never completely resist the temptation of offering something more broad, and when it does its "mythical" origins are even more discernible. The fact that myth retained, until much later than history, broader explanatory aspirations made it look less convincing in how it treated the particular details. The general conviction was that the mythical stories were, on the whole, not literally true (although sometimes they clearly were), that they were not referring to any particular historical events or if they were, the reference could not be, historically, very accurate. Therefore the conclusion would be that myth offers untrue stories, only ostensibly similar to the ones that history offers. But to claim that the truthfulness of myth is compromised because of that, would be rather misleading. It would also be difficult to use it as grounds for discounting the whole concept of myth. As it has been pointed out we can not speak of a "factual story unless we presuppose that it was constructed in one way or another."[26] The internal elements of a mythical story, or of any story that aspires to be factual, are parts of a narrative which employs various techniques and mechanisms in order to arrange its material. It wishes to contract or to expand, or perhaps even to exaggerate and provoke. A more free construction of the story was also a characteristic of the early stages of an activity when, as we have seen, it was still relatively more exploratory, curious and naïve, and less burdened with the strict consciousness of performing a distinct task. Primarily a story's narrative force comes from the arrangement of the available material in a manner which convinces of its coherence, truthfulness, potentiality and so forth. There may be various interpolations of features that are, or appear to be, superfluous but such elements do not necessarily dictate the narrative's cogency. More important, perhaps, than the arrangement of material is the selection of it. What makes something appropriate, suitable, and relevant, out of the infinite availability of 'things' to choose from, has been a fundamental problem for historical thinking. Finley maintained that "Long before anyone dreamed of history, myth gave an answer"[27] to this problem. The idea was that myth had already understood that selection implies focal points and certain themes on account of which the material acquires relevance, and it is around these points and themes that the material is then arranged. In that respect it was obvious that the mythical world was not random and constructed entirely by and in the myth-maker's imagination, but it had an internal coherence which was the result of the aforementioned process of selection and arrangement. The same process which has been used to create narratives accepted as historical. Ultimately no narrative can be universally convincing and an easy way to try and discount it would be to find internal inconsistencies and elements that perhaps do not belong there. But this can be a difficult task as material selection and arrangement are fundamental problems of narrative and their details can be elusive. Myth, therefore, was not doing something outrageously different than any historical narrative, and in fact it seems to have been there even before history itself. But while historical narratives have been often forgiven with only a mild rebuke for any suspicious treatment of the material, for myth the slightest deviation from the (quite vague and undefined) rules of composition (selection and arrangement) has been seen as a major transgression, calling into question the entire truthfulness and structure of the mythical story. But even this strict judgement reveals the affinity between history and myth, or the expectation that myth should or could have been even closer to history but it has failed to do so.

Occasionally the structure of myth was considered under a more positive light. Instead of the narrow task of describing and explaining the ephemeral historical reality, myth was thought of as offering a story which transcends those historical circumstances and presents something universal and eternal. A common conclusion has been that "mythology was a valuable method of universalizing the particular, of giving a transcendental meaning to the transient events and situations."[28] The danger of accepting this conclusion is that any possibility of a myth having historical value may collapse. The mythical story becomes an *exemplum*, a universal truth of some description but not a historical truth. Using the mythical story as a way to learn something about the specific society that produced such stories will not be very illuminating: the story could potentially be equally valid for any society. By universalising the particular the historical information is lost, the particular ceases to be particular and becomes a timeless point. No matter what truth this point may possess it is a generic, perhaps philosophical, truth and not a historical one. Ironically obtaining myth's truthfulness from the fact that it offers a universally valid story may also produce the opposite effect. In order for myth to become universally recognisable and valid it would have to undergo a process of allegorisation, to be treated in such a way as to extract what the various allegorical interpreters consider to be its valuable or most relevant features, which were hidden inside myth's convoluted narrative. It was partly due to such allegorising methods that gradually myth became synonymous with falsehood. For there is no absolute way to universalise something. To find the essence, in other words, of a story which will be able to turn all particular instances into universalities. Devoid of various crucial details the story will become unstable because the historical truth will be pushed to become an ideal form.

* * *

In a sense it will always be tempting to say that myth and history "in a very special sense, are interdependent... fertilise each other; and it is doubtful whether the one could exist without the other"[29] Both are nebulous spectacles of origins, of the formative steps of truthful and meaningful narratives and of the early impulses to describe, to record, to catalogue, to preserve, and to remember. Sometimes that may be seen as almost impious, but necessary, attempts to explain and provide the individual with a sense of divinity and immortality. But their scope was also much more modest. Out of the uncategorised mass or chaos they wished to indicate what is habitable and possible. They created possibilities for individual sovereignty in a universe which could be accepted as full of meaning. Man's gradual departure from myth was also a gradual loss of this special idea of freedom. In many significant ways the kind of mind which created myths is no longer present. Perhaps it has been replaced by something else or hopefully part of it still resides within history.

Notes

1 Croce, *Historiography*, 182.
2 Jaspers, *Origin and Goal of History*, 3.

3 Ibid.
4 Taylor Stevenson, *History as Myth*, 31.
5 Ibid., 45.
6 Vico, *The First New Science*, 149.
7 Ibid., 227.
8 Vico, *New Science*, 6.
9 Vico, *The First New Science*, 149.
10 Ibid.
11 Vico, *New Science*, 33.
12 Ibid., 44.
13 Haddock, *Introduction to Historical Thought*, 65.
14 Taylor Stevenson, *History as Myth*, 6.
15 Ibid., 5–6.
16 Ibid., 6.
17 Ibid.
18 Ibid.
19 Ibid.
20 Collingwood, *Idea of Nature*, 175.
21 Ibid., 177.
22 McNeill, *Mythistory*, 3.
23 Oakeshott, *Experience and its Modes*, 32.
24 Oakeshott, *Rationalism in Politics*, 137.
25 Munz, "Myth and History," 9.
26 Ibid., 5.
27 Finley, "Myth, Memory, History," 13.
28 Vessey, "Flavian Epic," 569.
29 Munz, "Myth and History," 1.

References

Collingwood, Robin George. *The Idea of Nature*. Oxford: Oxford Clarendon Press, 1945.

Croce, Benedetto. *Theory and History of Historiography*. Translated by Douglas Ainslie. London: George G. Harrap & Co. Ltd, 1921.

Finley, Moses Israel. "Myth, Memory and History." In *The Use and Abuse of History*, edited by Moses Israel Finley, 11–33. New York: The Viking Press, 1975.

Haddock, Bruce Anthony. *An Introduction to Historical Thought*. London: Edward Arnold Ltd, 1980.

Jaspers, Karl. *The Origin and Goal of History*, Translated by Michael Bullock. New Haven: Yale University Press, 1953.

McNeill, William Hardy. *Mythistory and Other Essays*. Chicago: The University of Chicago Press, 1986.

Munz, Peter. "History and Myth." *Philosophical Quarterly* 6, no. 22 (January 1956): 1–16.

Oakeshott, Michael. *Experience and Its Modes*. Cambridge: Cambridge University Press, 1933.

Oakeshott, Michael. *Rationalism in Politics and Other Essays*. London: Methuen & Co Ltd, 1962.

Vessey, D.W.T.C. "Flavian Epic." In *The Cambridge History of Classical Literature, II: Latin Literature*, edited by Edward John Kenney and Wendell Vernon Clausen, 558–596. Cambridge: Cambridge University Press, 1982.

Vico, Giambattista. *The New Science of Giambattista Vico*. Revised translation of the third edition [1744] by Thomas Goddard Bergin and Max Harold Fisch. Ithaca: Cornell University Press, 1968.

Vico, Giambattista. *The First New Science*, edited and translated by Leon Pompa. Cambridge: Cambridge University Press, 2002.

Taylor Stevenson, William. *History as Myth. The Import for Contemporary Theology*. New York: The Seabury Press, 1969.

Index

Acton, Lord 79
Aeschylus 11
Aetiological myth 31, 40n28
Allegorical interpretations of myths
    17, 20
Anthropology and myth 29, 30–1, 32,
    40n28
Anthropomorphism 6–7, 8
Aristotle 10–11
Athena and Poseidon contest 9

Burke, E: connection with Vico 46;
    and the Enlightenment 79; as
    historian and historical innovator
    79–83; and Romanticism 79–80; on
    religion 80–1
Butterfield, H. xi, 80

Collingwood, R.G. x, 19, 23–4,
    24n17, 26–38, 51–2, 69–70, 88
Croce, B. 80, 85
Chronology and myths 7–8, 10, 11

de Maistre, J. 78
Deism 21–2

Enlightenment: and history 51, 52,
    53–4, 69; against myth 45; and
    religion 21–3; and Renaissance
    69–70; and Romanticism 57, 63,
    64–5, 72
Ephorus 12
Epic poetry and bards 5, 6, 8, 11
Euhemerism/Euhemerus xiiin1,
    20, 85

Fairy tales as myths 27–32, 38
Frazer, J.G. 29, 31
Freud, S. 29, 31–2

Genealogies in myths 7–8, 11–12
Grimm, brothers 29
Grotius, H. 87

Hamann, J.G. 46
Hecataeus of Miletus 10, 12
Herodotus 6, 12
History and myth as activities 90–5
Historical change 59–64
Historical cosmopolitanism 64–8
Hume, D. 51, 80

Jaspers, K. 85
Jung, C. 29, 31–2
Jacobinism 80

Lord Acton; see Acton, Lord

Middle Ages/medieval period 36–7,
    51, 65, 69, 70, 72, 73, 79, 80
Müller, M. 29–30, 31, 32
Myths in antiquity 3–13
Myth and history as activities;
    see History and myth as activities
Mythistory xii, xiiin5

Origins of myths 90–5

Plato 10–11
Psychology and myths/fairy tales
    28, 31–2

Primitive: life/religion 30–6; man; *see* 'Savages'
Pufendorf, S. von 87

Realism in myth 6–7, 8
Religion: ancient European societies, myths and 21; Burke on 80–1; Collingwood and 26–7; Euhemerism and 20; totemism and 37; Voltaire and the Enlightenment against 21–2
Renaissance 48–9, 52, 69–70, 80
Romanticism: historical mindedness 51–9; meanings 47–51; political philosophy 71–4
Rituals and myths 31, 35–6, 40n28
Ruskin, J. 28–9, 39n5, 40n19

'Savages' 31–2

Science and scientific spirit: and history 33, 53–4, 57, 59, 88; and religion 23–4
Scott, Sir W. 51
Secularism 22–3, 65
Selden, J. 87

Theopompus 12
Thucydides 6, 12
Tylor, E.B. 29, 30–1

Unity of mind 68–71

Vico, G xi–xii, 19, 20, 21, 38, 46, 80, 81, 86–7
Voltaire 21–2, 58

Women and voting in antiquity 9